The Six Month Kingdom

Albania 1914

Captain Duncan Heaton-Armstrong

Edited by Gervase Belfield and Bejtullah Destani
With an Introduction by Gervase Belfield

I.B. TAURIS

LONDON · NEW YORK

in association with
THE CENTRE FOR ALBANIAN STUDIES

Published in 2005 by I.B.Tauris & Co. Ltd.
6 Salem Road,
London W2 4BU
175 Fifth Avenue, New York NY 10010
www.ibtauris.com

In association with
The Centre for Albanian Studies

In the United States of America and in Canada distributed by Palgrave
Macmillan, a division of St Martins Press, 175 Fifth Avenue, New York
NY 10010

ISBN: 1 85043 761 0
EAN: 978 1 85043 761 1

A full CIP record for this book is available from the British Library
A full CIP record for this book is available from the Library of Congress

Library of Congress catalog card: available

Printed and bound in Great Britain by TJ International Ltd, Padstow, Cornwall
using camera-ready copy edited and supplied by the editors.

Contents

EDITORIAL NOTES
AND ACKNOWLEDGEMENTS

. . . . .

Ever since I studied Balkan history at university in the mid-1970s, I have wanted to write a book about Albania, and the opportunity presented itself when my Albanian friend, historian and publisher, Bejtullah Destanti, suggested I edit the memoirs of Captain Duncan Heaton-Armstrong (1886-1969). For nearly nine months, between January and August 1914, Heaton-Armstrong held the post of "Private Secretary and Comptroller of the Privy Purse" to Prince William of Wied, a young German prince who had been persuaded by the six Great Powers of Europe to accept the throne of Albania. These memoirs were entitled The Six Month Kingdom; they give the most detailed narrative of the reign of Prince William of Wied known to exist.

It should be pointed out at once that, strictly speaking, throughout the period with which this book is concerned, Albania was not a kingdom, but a principality, and Prince William of Wied was not a king but remained a prince. My justification for calling him "King William" after he accepted the throne, and for calling Albania a kingdom, is two-fold. First, he was known to the Albanians as "Mbret" (and is often referred to as this by Heaton-Armstrong), which translates more closely into English as King than Prince. Secondly, he was generally known throughout Europe as "King William of Albania", and Heaton-Armstrong refers to the "King" and "Kingdom" of Albania throughout his memoirs.

The manuscript of the memoirs was given by Duncan Heaton-Armstrong's daughter, Mrs Griselda Adam, together with a photograph album and many press cuttings, to the Centre for Albanian Studies, which was set up by Bejtullah about ten years ago to publish source material relating to the history of Albania. Bejtullah suggested a very brief Introduction, but as I proceeded, I soon realised that both before and after King William accepted the throne, there lay an extraordinary story, most of which had never been told before. The intended "brief Introduction" rapidly grew into a book covering Albanian history between 1912 and the proclamation of a Republic by Ahmed Bey Zogu (the future King Zog) on 22 January 1925. Within this period, there were about 40 serious candidates for the throne, and at least as twice as many replied to an advertisement placed in the "Situations Vacant" section of a London newspaper, which read "Wanted, a King; an English country gentleman preferred – Apply to the Government of Albania". I hope to publish, as a separate book, the story of Albania's quest for a king.

There was little in the way of standardisation in the spelling of Albanian names of people and places. I have retained Heaton-Armstrong's naming of the main towns as they were generally known at the period in which he was writing. This is often different from the names now found on modern maps of the country. Thus, the former capital, Durazzo, is now known as Durres; Scutari is now known as Shkoder, and Valona as Vlora. As for the spelling of given names and surnames, I have followed the advice of Bejtullah. Albanian names are often complicated. For instance, King William's great enemy, Essad Pasha Toptani (1863-1920), was generally known as Essad Pasha. Essad was his given name; his surname Toptani was very rarely used. The name Pasha is a title derived from the Ottoman word for governor; it was not a surname. Similarly, "Bey" is a title used to denote a landowner. I have made very few alterations to the text of Duncan Heaton-Armstrong's manuscript, and have left some of his footnotes intact, but I have added more of my own to identify people and to explain places.

This project has, to a large extent, been a joint enterprise with Bejtullah, whose knowledge of Albanian history is unrivalled. Over the past year, a package has arrived almost every week on my doorstep from him containing some new and fascinatingly obscure source (often in Albanian, Italian or German), revealing another unlikely candidate for the throne or shedding fresh light on the reign of King William. His enthusiasm has been enormous, and my debt to him is large. I am grateful for information, advice and friendly encourage-ment from the Heaton-Armstrong family, particularly Duncan's great-nephew, Anthony Heaton-Armstrong, and Mrs Griselda Adam. I must also thank Mrs Marlis Hutchings for skilfully translating

William of Wied's Denkschrift uber Albanien into English. My wife, Drusilla, and our children must know more about the bye-ways of Albanian history than most families in Winchester, and I thank them for their forbearance.

The Centre for Albanian Studies gratefully acknowledges the assistance of Mrs Griselda Adam, Kosova Aid, Mr and Mrs Tanush Frasheri and Margaret and Pam Davis.

INTRODUCTION

. . . . .

By Gervase Belfield

Prince William of Wied

From the second half of the fifteenth-century until independence was declared on 28 November 1912, Albania was part of the Ottoman Empire. The country emerged very hesitantly into the modern world when, on 28 November 1912, its independence was proclaimed at the port of Valona (now called Vlora) by its 68 year old nationalist leader, Ismail Kemal Vlora (1844-1919). Left to themselves the Albanian leaders would have preferred another twenty years, at least, to prepare their nation for independence, under the nominal suzerainty of the Sultan of Turkey. The country was a desperately poor and neglected backwater. King William arrived in 1914 to find no railways, appallingly bad roads and communications, few public buildings or schools and no university. There was no police force outside the towns, and Albania was famous for its blood feuds. It had no currency or banks, and the economy was primitive and almost entirely agricultural.

Albania was the creation of the Great Powers, particularly Austria-Hungary and Italy; without their intervention in 1913 at the end of the First Balkan War, the Ottoman province of Albania would have divided up between its victorious neighbours, the Greeks to the south, the Serbs to the east and the Montenegrins to the north. From December 1912, for nearly a year, the ambassadors in London of the six Great Powers of Europe (Britain, France, Germany, Russia, Austria-Hungary and Italy), under the chairmanship of the British Foreign Secretary, Sir Edward Grey, met regularly to fashion the new state of Albania into a shape which would be acceptable to all the powers. Albanians played no part in the selection of their future

monarch, just as they played no part in the definition of their borders
or the construction of their constitution. About a third of the territory
in which Albanians formed the majority of the population, mainly the
province of Kosovo, was given to the Serbs, the Montenegrins and the
Greeks. The Great Powers sanctioned the creation of a truncated
Albania not because of any modern belief in "the right to self-
determination" of a small nation, but because it was believed that an
Albanian state was essential to preserve the fragile peace in Europe.
Albania was created to serve a specific political objective. On 29 July
1913 the Conference of Ambassadors formally announced that
Albania would be an independent and neutral principality (not a
kingdom), its security guaranteed by the Great Powers. It was
promised that a prince would be appointed within six months. The
European statesmen who fashioned the country had no detailed
knowledge of it, nor did they consider very closely what sort of
monarch the Albanians either desired or required. The selection of a
prince was yet another headache for the foreign ministries; each of the
many candidates seemed to have an insurmountable defect in the eyes
of one or other of the Great Powers. Personal qualities and abilities
were hardly considered; the imperative factor was to find a man
without any impediment in terms of nationality or religion; one who
would not contribute further to international tensions. As for the
Albanians, they had little appreciation of the complex web of
diplomatic manoeuvring and subtle intrigue in the chancelleries of
Europe. In so far as they had any view on the subject, many would
have preferred a prince from the British royal family; Prince Arthur,
Duke of Connaught (1850-1942), the third son of Queen Victoria,
was probably the favourite (Edith Durham, Albania and the
Albanians, page 88, and Twenty Years of Balkan Tangle, page 257).
Many other Albanians would have liked a Moslem prince rather than
a Christian one, this being a reflection of the fact that two thirds of
the population was Moslem. They were certainly impatient with the
Great Powers for their slowness in selecting a prince, but equally they
were immensely grateful to them for taking on this role; like an
orphaned child, they longed for the stability and prestige of a parent
they could call their own.

By September 1913 still no prince had been announced. Europe
had now divided firmly into two diplomatic and military camps,
Germany and Austria-Hungary on the one hand, and the Entente
Cordial between Great Britain and France, supported by Russia, on

the other. The Austro-Hungarians, who took the initiative in recruiting a prince, would certainly not have accepted an Italian or a French candidate, and would probably have opposed a British prince or aristocrat. The Italians, who were equally keen to gain influence in Albania, preferred to see a Protestant on the throne and would certainly not have agreed to any prince from Austria-Hungary or its Catholic allies in southern Germany. The Russians would also have objected to a Catholic prince, and tended to favour a Moslem. Most leading Albanians would have ruled out a Moslem, a Catholic or an Orthodox prince, because significant proportions of the Albanian population would have been alienated by any one of these. Their desire for a British prince could not be fulfilled. The room for manoeuvre was not great. Ideally the candidate needed to be a distinguished Protestant prince with connections to several royal houses and with many robust personal virtues, capable of strong military leadership, having a good understanding of international diplomacy, and above all giving complete dedication to the cause of a desperately poor and vulnerable small nation, emerging from centuries of stagnation under the Ottoman empire.

When it was announced, in November 1913, that His Serene Highness Prince William Frederick Henry of Wied, had been selected by the Great Powers to be the future sovereign, there was great optimism in Albania, and throughout the capitals of Europe, that a man with most of these virtues had at last been found. Prince William was then a 37 year old Captain in the 3rd Regiment of Uhlans of the Guard, in the imperial German army. He was tall, handsome and imposing; he was known as a capable soldier, popular with both his fellow officers in Potsdam and with society in Berlin. He was Protestant by religion and well connected, particularly to the Dutch and Prussian royal families. He was married to an attractive and vivacious princess, and they had two young children, Princess Maria Eleanora, then nearly four, and a son and heir, Prince Carol Victor, who was six months.

The Princes of Wied were minor German royalty, closer in social status to the higher reaches of the aristocracy than to dynasties such the Habsburgs and Hohenzollerns. Prince William was born at the family seat at Neuwied, overlooking the River Rhine, near Koblenz, on 26 March 1876, the second son of His Serene Highness William, 5th Prince of Wied (1845-1907) and his wife, Princess Marie of the Netherlands (1841-1910). Throughout his youth his father's sister, the extremely eccentric and highly-strung Queen Elisabeth of Roumania (1843-1916), was an important influence on William. The Wied family used to spend "happy weeks" at Pelesc Castle, the royal residence at Sinaia in the Transylvanian Alps in Roumania. Elizabeth was a striking figure: tall and plump, with bright blue eyes and prematurely white hair. Writing was the main outlet for her huge energy, and she wrote over 50 books under the pen-name "Carmen Sylva" (Song and Nature); her oeuvre was eclectic: verses with easy rhythms, often expressing nostalgia for her homeland on the Rhine, folk-tales, Roumanian literature and folk-law, and reminiscences. She lived a life of great emotional intensity; her successor as Queen of Roumania described her as "both splendid and absurd". In complete contrast, her husband King Carol I (died 1914), was an extremely efficient and hard-working man.

On 30 November 1906 Prince William of Wied married Princess Sophie Helene Cecilie, the 21 year-old daughter of Victor, Hereditary Prince of Schonburg-Waldenburg (died 1888), and his wife, Princess Lucy (died 1903). Sophie was born on 21 May 1885 in Potsdam, and spent most of her youth in Moldavia, Roumania, where her mother's family had a country house and estate called Fantanele. She was a much loved protégé and close companion of Queen Elisabeth; together they sang, painted, wrote poetry, and played the harp; they spoke to mystical spirits beyond this world. Sophie and Elisabeth saw in Albania a thrilling and glamorous adventure. The hesitant Prince William of Wied was cajoled by his wife and aunt, and bullied, behind the scenes, by the Austro-Hungarians into accepting the throne. In his brief memoirs (Denkschrift uber Albanien), he says that for nearly six months after he first turned down the throne in the spring of 1913, the Austrians put increasing pressure on him to change his mind. He relented, probably during a visit to Sinaia in September 1913. Roumania was a convenient stage-entrance from which he could emerge as a "neutral" candidate. He was acceptable to the all Great Powers above all because nobody objected to him. He had no previous connection with, or knowledge of, Albania. A contemporary described William as "a fine, healthy, kindly fellow, with a soft voice and a wide smile, but not having the artistic temperament, he was occasionally somewhat bewildered by the atmosphere into which he was being drawn ... Sophie was full of excited anticipation, but it seemed ... as though quiet William was a little less enthusiastic, not being so deeply moved by the romantic possibilities of this new career." (Queen Marie of Roumania, The Story of My Life, vol 2, p 295). Queen Elisabeth launched a vigorous campaign in the Viennese newspapers in favour of William's candidature for the throne, starting with an article entitled "Fairyland wants its Prince". This described how the Albanians clamoured for a sovereign, and, in romantic Wagnerian prose, introduced a scion of an ancient race dwelling on the banks of the river Rhine (The Memoirs of Ismail Kemal Bey, page 379). Emperor William II of Germany, who took a close interest in his kinsman, was in no doubt who lay behind the Prince's eventual acceptance of the throne: "The ambitious, mystically excited wife of the prince saw in Albania the fulfilment of her wishes, and 'Ce que femme veut, Dieu le veut'", the Emperor wrote in his memoirs (Ex-Kaiser Wilhelm II, My Memoirs, 1879-1918, page 162).

His naivety, and lack of experience in diplomacy and politics showed itself during the long and tortuous diplomatic process by which William came to be formally offered the throne. In particular, it was vital that he should not be presented as the preferred candidate of any one power, but the unanimous choice of all. Although German by nationality, the German government distanced itself from the whole project, while the Emperor was openly hostile to the whole adventure. Guided by his uncle, King Carol of Roumania, William negotiated the terms upon which he would accept the throne. A substantial loan of 10 million French francs was promised to him, but he made the crucial mistake of not insisting upon a military force to accompany him to Albania to guarantee the disputed borders of the new country, and its internal security. Eventually, on 7 February 1914 William sent a formal note to the ambassadors of the Great Powers in Berlin, stating that he had decided to accept the throne of Albania and would proceed there shortly.

Meanwhile, in Albania news of William of Wied's candidature was received with mixed feelings. Its leaders urged the Great Powers to install him as quickly as possible. The young Roman Catholic Albanian diplomat, Philip Nogga, was allegedly paid 30,000 French francs by the Roumanian government to promote Wied's cause in Albania and elsewhere; he was in Valona in about September 1913, distributing picture post-cards of the Prince, small mementoes, and even money. Ismail Kemal, the head of Provisional Government, was unenthusiastic, accusing Queen Elisabeth of promoting her nephew through bribery: "The prospect of confiding the destinies of Albania to this unknown celebrity did not particularly enchant me, but what troubled me more was the propaganda that began openly in favour of this candidature, in which money and presents were distributed with cynical effrontery" (The Memoirs of Ismail Kemal Bey, page 379). It is easy to understand the mutual lack of enthusiasm. Germany and its people had no interests, political or economic, in Albania; William was a completely unknown quantity. Kemal's government was beset with problems, the greatest of which was Essad Pasha, who set up his own rival administration in central Albania in the autumn of 1913. In January 1914 both men were implicated in a serious plot to restore the country to Ottoman rule, and install a Turkish prince as ruler. The Great Powers intervened, and set up an "International Commission of Control" as an interim administration until the new monarch arrived. This consisted of a representative of each of the Great Powers, and one Albanian. They were joined by 15 Dutch army officers, whose main task was to recruit and train, from scratch, an Albanian army. In fact, these brave men, who feature so prominently in Heaton-Armstrong's narrative, bore the brunt of the fighting during King William's reign, and the ablest, Colonel Lodewijk Thomson, was killed in action on 15 June 1914.

William's protracted negotiations with the Great Powers left him little time to learn about his new kingdom. Many of the people who tried to help him commented on his lack of preparation for the task before him. For instance Emperor William drew the Prince's attention to a pamphlet which had just been published by an Austrian General Staff Officer, giving an account of his recent travels in Albania. The officer pointed out that any future ruler should not reside on the coast close to the protection of the warships of the Powers, but should show himself to the people by travelling around on horseback in a nomadic style, with a "bag of sequins". He should bind himself to the clan leaders, since there was no regular army in Albania. "Did the Prince ever read the pamphlet?" asked the Emperor; the answer was clearly not: "he adopted a course contrary to its advice and my advice" (My Memoirs, page 163). A retired German army officer, Colonel William Shaefer, who knew the country well, met William and Sophie in January 1914, and stated "I was taken aback by their absolute ignorance about everything Albanian or Eastern ... Both the Prince and Princess looked very miserable at having to go to Albania... The Princess seemed to be gifted with a finer perception, but looked a nervous person" (National Archives (NA) ref : FO371/1892). The Wieds reported to their English friend, Aubrey Herbert MP (1880-

1923) who knew Albania and Albanian better than any other Englishman of his day, that they were finding the language "pretty stiff work ... We feel almost like children learning geography and all sorts of things one has not learnt for centuries. We see heaps of anxieties and dangers for the future, but we try to see the beautiful and interesting side, as well ..." (Somerset Record Office ref : DD/HER/34).

The popular press of Western Europe presented the new dynasty in an entirely different light; it was as if Ruritania had come to life, and the great Albanian adventure of the Wied family was reported in great detail. For instance, the Daily Mail of 21 January 1914, portrayed William as "Lohengrin" after the heroic knight in Wagner's opera; the article described him as having been "a brilliant undergraduate" at Jena University (in fact he left without taking a degree); he was also the "strongest man in the university", capable of lifting a comrade high in the air with one arm. He was full of "burning desire to face the ominous uncertainties of the new kingdom ... He is ready to beard a world of dangers unseen". Princess Sophie's beauty and charms were also extolled: "She was brought up not to be afraid of common people". Together "they will never found lacking in pluck".

The reign of King William was a catalogue of disasters and misfortunes, starting with the serious rebellion fermented by the Greeks in Epirus, along the southern border of Albania in April 1914. This was followed by an uprising of Moslems, with a medley of grievances, in central Albania, which rapidly turned into a movement to overthrow William in favour of a Moslem prince. William's weak government never came close to suppressing either of these threats, and he failed to establish any effective rule in the country at large. Few commentators have disagreed that William of Wied was a well-meaning and honourable man, and he would, no doubt, have made a good constitutional figurehead in the tranquil setting of a modern western European monarchy. But he was totally unsuited to the role which he reluctantly agreed to take on in Albania. Although he was superficially charming, he had a formal, rather wooden approach to kingship, which was perhaps a reflection of his somewhat limited military mind. He was lacking in imagination and energy, and as Duncan Heaton-Armstrong emphasises, he was extremely indecisive. In his memoirs, he admits that he made some mistakes and had insufficient knowledge of the country and its people. He expected the loyalty and devotion of his subjects almost as a matter of course, and seemed genuinely surprised at the duplicity and cunning of Essad Pasha, whose malign influence dominated the first half of his reign. With the benefit of hindsight, King William identified Essad as being at the root of his misfortunes; he described him as "brutal" and "illiterate (apart from laboriously scribbling his name)". (Denkschrift, pages 10-11) William also believed, as did most other commentators, probably correctly although no certain proof exists, that Essad was at various points in the reign, in the pay of the Serbs, the Montenegrins, the Italians and the Greeks. One obvious illustration of Essad's manipulation of the royal family was his advice to them as soon as they arrived in Albania not to venture out of Durazzo. William's height and imposing military bearing would have appealed to Albanians, who liked their leaders and chieftains to be visible and physically impressive. William singularly failed to capitalise upon this great natural asset; instead of immediately touring the country and meeting its people, he rarely ventured out the confines of the palace at Durazzo. During his entire reign he spent just one night away from the palace, on board the Italian ship "Misurata" en route to Valona, where he and Queen Sophie spent the day on 26 July 1914. When the intrepid Englishwoman Edith Durham (1863-1944) who, from about 1905, devoted most of her life to the Albanians, met Queen Sophie, she tackled her on this issue; she begged them "to go to Valona or Scutari, and at once start a tour through the land. I offered to go with her, and assured her safe conduct, saying all misunderstanding would have been avoided had she and the Prince made such a journey on arrival. She said she had wished to, but that Essad always advised against it". (Balkan Tangle, page 267-8). William claimed he was filled with high regard for the Germanic virtues of "Right, Justice and Truthfulness, and did not possess the armoury to fend off the lies, malice and intrigues of the Serbs and Italians" (Denkschrift page 51). He lacked the flamboyance and nerve of his fellow countryman, Baron Theodore von Neuhoff, who in 1736, persuaded the Corsicans to crown him as their King, and who also reigned for only six months.

King William left Albania on 3 September 1914, a completely discredited figure in Albania and throughout Europe. The Great War had started, and his departure went unnoticed. Yet he never abdicated, and for the next 30 years, until his death on 18 April 1945, he retained an almost child-like belief that he might be restored, or that his son might be given a chance to rule Albania. A month after his departure, he was shocked to learn that Essad had broken his word of honour as an officer not to return to Albania without his permission. Essad was welcomed back to Durazzo with great ostentation and publicity by the Italians, and he installed himself in the Wied family's private rooms in the palace, which the Moslem rebels had preserved untouched. William wrote to Essad requesting the return of his family property, but Essad replied with a demand for half a million marks; "naturally I refused Essad, so he sold or gave away the greatest part of my personal valuables, horses, carriages, silver, works of art etc.... Only the Austrian consul managed to preserve a few family heirlooms" (Denkschrift, page 32). Queen Sophie was particularly upset at the loss of her favourite harp.

At the beginning of 1916 the Austrians were successful in driving out the Serbs and Montenegrins from the whole of the northern half of Albania. This gave William hope that he would be restored as King of Albania. In the following year, on 3 June 1917, Italy's ambition to dominate Albania caused her to proclaim the country an Italian Protectorate, and this event drew forth "the sharpest protest" from William in his brief memoirs, entitled Denkschrift uber Albanien, which were published in August 1917. This booklet might more accurately be described as a political memorandum, or reflections on the politics of his brief reign and subsequent developments in Albania. Its true purpose was undoubtedly to persuade the Austro-Hungarian government to give him a second chance in Albania. He still saw himself as the only legitimate ruler of the country, selected and guaranteed by all the Great Powers; he had no intention of abdicating. Why, now that the situation was again favourable to him, in northern Albania at least, were the Austrians no longer interested in supporting him? When he had arrived in Albania in March 1914, he had not realised the true extent of the problems facing the country, but now more than three years later, he claimed he had far greater knowledge and insight into his country, drawn from practical experience.

William stated that throughout the war, wherever he was serving "I was continually thinking of Albania. During my leave from the battle-front, I worked for my country as best I could and attempted to keep in touch with Albanians inside and outside the country" (Denkschrift, page 38). Queen Sophie, too, never lost her enthusiasm for Albania; according to Queen Marie of Roumania, writing in the early 1930s, "Sophie has kept her love for Albania and the Albanians; the romance of that wild country sank into her soul and still lives there; the flame of her enthusiasm has not burnt out ..." (Marie,

Queen of Roumania, Story of My Life, vol 2, page 295).

The defeat of Germany at the end of 1918 effectively ended William of Wied's chances of being restored to his throne; his active military service in the German army during the Great War alone would have disqualified him. On the other hand, the leading Albanian politician at the end of the war, Akif Pasha Elbasani, told a British Foreign Office official in April 1919 that he and many others wished to return to the "starting point government" established by the Great Powers under Wied, since it was the only "National Government" the Albanians had ever had. Akif described how, in a primitive people, the sentiment of loyalty is deep, and there was considerable sympathy for Wied personally "as an unfortunate man who was driven from the land by foreign intrigues". Since William had not abdicated, he was still the rightful ruler of the country; if the Great Powers found him unacceptable, they should persuade him to renounce the throne and select another in his place (NA ref: FO608/29). The question of whether Albania should retain its monarchy or become a republic was discussed in January 1920 at the important National Congress held in the town of Lushnja, under the leadership of Akif. The deputies at Lushnja decided in favour of the former, but postponed any discussion of who might be offered the throne until the country was more secure. They then elected a High Council of Regency, consisting of four members, each representing a different strand of religion, these being two Moslems, one from the mild Bektashi sect and one from the stricter Sunni sect, a Roman Catholic and an Orthodox Christian. The senior member or President of this High Council was Akif Pasha Elbasani. The powers of the Council were limited and were never clearly defined, although they had an important role in calling elections and in forming cabinets. The four Regents were popularly referred to as "the quarter kings", and this curious, if not unique, constitutional quadruped remained the nominal head of state for five years until January 1925, when Ahmed Bey Zogu led a coup and proclaimed a Republic.

When Zogu changed the Albanian constitution in August 1928, and was proclaimed King Zog of the Albanians on 1 September, William of Wied emerged briefly from the shadows and issued a formal protest from Berlin. He said that he "claims for himself and his heirs all the rights to the Albanian Throne to which he was elected in February 1914". He believed that the majority of Albanians still supported him, but considered that a free and unbiased referendum on the question of his return was at this point impossible. He was free from personal ambition; thought only of the welfare of his people, and awaited "the right moment" for his return (Times, 25 August 1928). In the following year, 1929, an Englishman, Joseph Swire, published his authoritative and detailed history of Albania (Albania – The Rise of a Kingdom, London, 1929), and acknowledged that William had discussed his reign "with the utmost frankness and provided me with a mass of valuable notes". Swire presented William and his reign in as generous a light as the facts would allow, and even suggested that should King Zog die without an heir, William might be restored.

In their private lives between the wars, the Wied family settled near Munich, where they lived modestly; in 1937 Swire reported that William enjoyed simple pleasures and drove his own car. The family also regularly visited Sophie's family castle and estate, Fantanele, near the town of Bacau, about 150 miles north of Bucharest, in Moldavia. Shooting and hunting remained William's main activity, but he never gave up hope of returning as King of Albania. In May 1935 King Carol II of Roumania invited him to attend the Conference of the Balkan Pact, which took place in Bucharest, even though Albania was not a party to the Pact. William was accorded "the usual royal honours" and his presence "has roused the most excited discussion in Balkan diplomatic circles". Here, in his "modest six-shilling-a-day" bedroom in a busy commercial hotel in Bucharest Prince William gave a lengthy interview to the Daily Mail's correspondent, who described him as "a magnificent figure of a sportsman and athlete, dressed in brown tweeds, strong and upstanding although 59 years of age". He claimed wistfully that he remembered every incident of his reign vividly; "I can never forget nor cease to admire the Albanian people. I made many friends among them, and I have never lost touch with my country. Especially I admire the mountaineers of the north and south – fearless, independent men of unswerving loyalty and attachment". He reiterated that he had never abdicated; "When I left the country in 1914, I promised then I would come back if ever they wanted me. If my people want me, I will go back at any time." (Daily Mail, 30 May 1935).

Sophie died aged 51 on 3 February 1936 at Fantanele. William survived another nine years; he died on 18 April 1945 at Predeal, near Sinaia, in Roumania. His death, which occurred near the end of the Second World War, appears to have gone un-noticed in the European and Albanian press. William and Sophie's two children took little more than a passing interest in Albania, although in his interview with the Daily Mail in May 1935, William hoped that one day his 22 year old son would be King. Prince Carol Victor studied law at Tubingen University in Germany; his doctoral thesis on criminal procedure was published in Stuttgart in 1936. He was a keen swordsman and enjoyed skiing; in 1937 Swire described him as a young man of great ability, with his father's good nature (Swire, Zog's Albania, page 202). During the Second World War, he served as an officer in the German army in Roumania, and in the autumn of 1941 there was speculation that the Germans, who had occupied Yugoslavia including the northern part of Kosovo, would use him to rally Albanians to the German cause. This worried Mussolini's Foreign Minister, Count Ciano, to such an extent that in November 1941, he accused the Germans of aiming to construct a new Albanian state led by Prince Carol Victor, which would be anti-Italian and whose militia would take a oath directly to Hitler. There appeared to be little truth to Ciano's fears, and the Germans reassured him they had no such ambitions for the prince (Fischer, Albania at War, 1939–1945, page 86). On the death of his father Carol Victor made no public claim to the throne of Albania. In September 1966, he married a widowed Englishwoman, Mrs Eileen de Coppet, the daughter of George Johnson. She was born in Chester in 1922, and she and Prince Carol Victor lived in Cheyne Walk, Chelsea, London. He died childless in Munich on 8 December 1973, aged 60, and was buried at Neuwied. Eileen died on 1 September 1985 in New York.

Princess Marie Eleanora, who as a four-year child in 1914 can be seen in many photographs of the Albanian royal family, studied economics in Berlin, following which she published a book about foreign investment and economics in South America (Das Auslandskapital in Sudamerika, Waldenburg, 1937). She was married twice; her first husband was her distant cousin, Prince Alfred Schonburg-Waldenburg, who died of an illness while on military service at Zeite, Germany, in 1941 after only four years of marriage. Her second husband, whom she married in Bucharest in February 1948, was a Roumanian politician and businessman, Jon Bunea. In the previous year, King Michael of Roumania was forced to abdicate and a Communist People's Republic was proclaimed. This created great danger for those with royal backgrounds, such as Princess Marie Eleanora, and she obtained employment in the press office of the British Legation in Bucharest, and was known as Mrs Bunea. This offered her no protection, since in the summer of 1949 she and her husband were arrested, and in March 1950 they were each sentenced to 15 years' hard labour. She spent more than six years in a prison for political prisoners. According to information given by a British woman who was released from a Roumanian prison, the Princess became ill and needed an operation, but the authority to move her from the prison to hospital in Miercurea Ciur took so long to arrive that the operation was unsuccessful, and she died childless on 28 or 30 September 1956. She was buried in the town cemetery at Miercurea Ciur. The Princess had left her possessions, such jewellery, watches, carpets and 300 gold sovereigns, at the British Legation in Bucharest while working there, and there is a file in the National Archives in London which notes that since the fate of her husband was unknown, these were held by friends at least until the early 1960s (FO371/128966).

The Heaton-Armstrong Brothers

Captain Duncan Heaton-Armstrong writes his eye-witness account of events in Albania in the first eight months of 1914 with vibrancy, directness, informality and humour, all of which reflect his engaging and irreverent character. His style may lack literary polish, but it is readable and well suited to the exciting story he has to tell. Most members of his social class and generation were taught from an early age to write lucidly and accurately, and Heaton-Armstrong was no exception. His memoirs show that he shared some of the prejudices of his generation and class, and his writing sometimes reveals a patronising attitude towards "native" Albanians.

He was born on 29 September 1886 at his mother's family home at Velden, in Austria close to the borders with Slovenia and Italy, the elder of two brothers, his younger brother being John Dunamace, known as "Jack". They were the sons of William Charles Heaton-Armstrong and his Austrian wife, Bertha, daughter of Baron Zois-Edelstein of Chateau d'Egg, Velden, Austria. William Charles had a strong buccaneering spirit and pursued various careers in several different countries; the story of his life reads like a novel by Joseph Conrad or John Buchan. He was born in 1853 at Gmunden, Austria, and was educated partly in Austria and partly in Ireland. In his youth, he fell out with his family and ran away to sea to join the British merchant navy, serving mainly in China and the Caribbean. With the help of his wealthy Austrian cousins, he was able to start trading by using spare space in the cargo holds to carry goods which he would then sell at a profit. Later his entrepreneurial spirit led him to import German beer into England, and he became very wealthy. Among his adventures, he joined the Turkish Navy during the Russo-Turkish War of 1876, and in the early 1880s he took out a warship from England for the Chilean navy during the Chilean-Peruvian War, and ran the gauntlet of a Peruvian blockade of the South American coast.

After his marriage in 1885 William Charles lived partly in Austria and partly in London. In the 1890s, he developed an interest in Irish politics, and stood as a Conservative candidate for mid-Tipperary in 1892. He failed to gain the seat, and thereafter changed his allegiance to the English Liberal party, and in 1906 was elected as Member of Parliament for Sudbury, Suffolk. He sat until he retired from politics in January 1910. He then pursued a career as a banker, and as such helped to finance railways in Jersey and in British Columbia, Canada, where a town was named after him. However, his banking career ended in financial disaster during the First World War. He died in July 1917, and his widow Bertha in December 1949.

Duncan and Jack had aristocratic Austrian blood and connections from two generations of maternal ancestors, and they were as much at home in Austria and middle Europe as they were in England or Ireland. In their paternal ancestry, they descended from Sir Thomas Armstrong (died 1662) who, like so many of his descendants, was a reckless adventurer, making his name as a royalist soldier in Ireland in the mid-seventeenth century. He was rewarded well for his loyalty to King Charles II, and was given the concession to mint farthings in Ireland. His descendants settled in County Tipperary, and served as members of parliament for the county. Sir Thomas's great grandson, Colonel William Armstrong MP, married the heiress, Mary Heaton of Mount Heaton in County Offaly, in 1731, and thereafter the family rose to be among the more substantial gentry in the southern midlands of Ireland. A century later, however, in 1834, the head of the family dissipated his huge fortune through gambling, and was forced to sell all his estates. He retired to the continent, thus beginning the links with Austria.

Duncan and Jack Heaton-Armstrong were both sent to school at Eton in 1900, but Duncan was unhappy, and only stayed three years. He was certainly not academic or intellectual, either by inclination or background, and after he left school his ambition was to join the army.

In 1904 he joined the 3rd battalion of the Lancashire Fusiliers as a militiaman (or part-time soldier) while receiving coaching for the army examinations. He appears to have changed direction since at the end of this year he went up to Cambridge, in the hope of gaining a place as an undergraduate; he made two unsuccessful attempts to pass the entrance examination at Trinity College. He admitted that his father gave him a good allowance, which meant he was able to entertain his friends lavishly, and to hunt with the Cambridge Harriers and the Fitzwilliam Hunt; according to family tradition he attended only one lecture, clothed in full hunting dress. After Cambridge, it was decided that he should try for the diplomatic service, and to this end he spent a year in France, followed by a year in Italy, to learn their languages. As with his other ambitions, however, his devotion to country sports handicapped his efforts to pass the entrance examinations.

His younger brother, Jack Heaton-Armstrong, who joined Duncan in Albania throughout the month of June 1914, was born in February 1888 at Edmonton, north London. He was of a more academic temperament, and gained a degree at Trinity, Cambridge. He then joined the Inner Temple in London, where he trained as a barrister, and was called to the bar in 1912. The Heaton-Armstrong brothers thus belong to that generation which, being under the age of 30 when the First World War began, saw many of their contemporaries killed or wounded.

Duncan begins his narrative by relating how, almost casually, he came to be appointed Private Secretary and Comptroller of the Privy Purse to Prince William of Wied on 7 January 1914. Before this date, he knew nothing about Albania, and it was purely his sense of adventure which prompted him to apply, along with 500 others, for the post. He claims that he accepted the job because he was "on the look out for a more stable career", but the pay, which was 30 shillings a month, could not have been an inducement. In fact, his cosmopolitan family background made him a very good choice to be the Prince's right-hand man. As a Protestant Irishman, his neutrality in the Balkans was an obvious advantage, but he spoke German "like a native", and was a first class interpreter in French and Italian. During the busy month of February 1914, as Prince William made his rapid tour of the European capitals, Duncan Heaton-Armstrong was frequently noticed in the popular press as the new king's private secretary, unofficial equerry, political lieutenant, press spokesman and general "handy man". The Tatler reported that Duncan's appointment caused a "good deal of flutter in Pan-German dovecotes", and in an interview with the Standard of 19 February, Duncan gave an account of King William's European tour and told how the old Turkish government headquarters (or Konak) in Durazzo were being renovated and equipped with electric lights and bathrooms to make them into an acceptable royal palace.

When the new royal family at last arrived at Durazzo on 9 March 1914, Harry (later Sir Harry) Lamb, the British representative in Albania on the International Commission of Control, was impressed by King William personally, but was critical of the various courtiers and advisers, both Albanian and European, including Duncan Heaton-Armstrong, who had been recruited to serve him. The Comptroller of the royal household, the Prussian Major von Trotha, was a typical "Junker", while the court doctor, Berghausen, was "a charlatan". However, Lamb's opinion of Duncan appears to have improved as he got to know him better; at the end of May 1914 he was impressed by Duncan's courage in the face of serious intimidation by the Italians, and he reported to Sir Edward Grey that Duncan was "one of the few independent sources of information and advice" (FO371 1895, page 43). For most of the reign, Duncan was also on very good terms with the King; the Daily Express (18 June 1914) reported that "he enjoyed the confidence of the unfortunate Mbret (Albanian King) to a charming degree. ... it is the custom of the Mbret almost every night to stroll into the officer's apartments (which adjoin his at the Palace) after the day's work, and there, over a pipe, discuss with his trusted secretary the latest doings in his somewhat troublous (sic) little state". The relationship only deteriorated at the end of the reign, caused, no doubt, by the stresses of having lived for three months with constant gun-fire within ear-shot of the palace, and the real threat of being over-run by the Moslem rebels. In addition, Britain and Germany declared war on 4 August, and the harmony which had prevailed between Duncan and his German employer and colleagues was put under great strain, and made his position at court virtually impossible.

Duncan's relations with Queen Sophie were not as good, and he grew to resent her "regal" manner towards him, particularly since he considered his own family as not much socially inferior to hers. We have a brief glimpse of Duncan's activities as a courtier in the memoirs of a Scottish missionary, Miss Katherine Stuart Macqueen, who arrived in Durazzo on 1 May 1914. She described him as "youthful, very free and easy and rather blunt ..." (Records of a Scotswoman, page 146). Miss Macqueen had several interviews and meetings with Queen Sophie, which were arranged by Duncan. The Queen was keen to offer Miss Macqueen a paid job organising industrial work for Albanian women, or running orphanages and hospitals : "Well, I told Captain Armstrong that if they paid my expenses and gave me a salary of £3 a week I would take the job. It was not meant that I should live in the Palace, he said, it was over-crowded, three of them sharing one room.... I suggested to Captain Armstrong that they might like some references. He said he didn't think they would bother about references – they didn't take up his!". After some negotiation with Duncan, it was agreed that the Albanian government could not afford to employ Miss Macqueen. During the first fortnight of May, however, she visited the palace most days, where she sat with the Queen and the two German ladies in waiting, cutting out and sewing clothes for the Albanian refugees who had fled from the Greeks in Epirus. She found Queen Sophie very easy and pleasant; "she is full of ideas for helping the people and especially about women's work, hospitals etc". Miss Macqueen's final comment on Albania was "Oh! It is an extraordinary little place, like an Anthony Hope kingdom" (Records of a Scotswoman, pages 145 to 153).

The hostile actions of the Greeks in southern Albania in May 1914 were the subject of much indignation at King William's court in Durazzo, and Duncan felt strongly enough to attempt a diplomatic initiative of his own, to which he did not refer in his memoirs. On 15 May he wrote to the British ambassador in Athens, Sir Francis Elliot, asking him to bring to the notice of the British government the "infamous conduct of the Greek government", and the atrocities committed by Greek soldiers in Epirus against Albanians. Duncan said he was writing the letter not in his capacity as secretary to the King of Albania, but as a British officer seconded to Albania under the Foreign Office for two years. Elliot acknowledged the letter, but was unsure as to how to respond to this unorthodox diplomatic communication. He forwarded Duncan's letter to the Foreign Office in London, and they replied that Elliot should take no notice of Heaton-Armstrong's "pardonable attempt to find a remedy". He was inexperienced, and furthermore was inaccurate in describing himself as "seconded under the Foreign Office"; he was in fact "an officer of the Special Reserve, seconded in his Regiment for service under the

Albanian government, and he has no connection with the Foreign Office." (FO371 1888, page 227-30).

From the end of May onwards, Duncan's main pre-occupations were military rather than diplomatic or courtly. For instance, between 18 and 22 May he made urgent attempts to recruit contingents of Catholic soldiers from the "Malissori" tribes of northern Albania to help quell the Moslem rebellion against King William. This rebellion reached a climax in the middle of June; both Heaton-Armstrong brothers were noted for their courage and initiative in the fierce fighting; indeed their heroic exploits were widely reported in the British press throughout June and July. For instance, on 18 June 1914, the front page of the Daily Sketch was devoted entirely to Duncan; beneath the caption "Captain Armstrong, the British Officer who keeps the Albanian King on his throne, makes the rebels show a white flag", two photographs of him were printed, one in the splendid Albanian blue-grey cavalry uniform with black facings and astrakhan cap, topped with a tall aigrette, which he wore on formal occasions in Albania. The report described him as "another British officer seeking adventure in troublesome foreign parts and finding fame ... It was Captain Heaton-Armstrong who tapped Essad Pasha on the shoulder, and saying 'Come with me', marched him off under fire as a captive when it was found that he was scheming to overthrow the new King". The following day, a friend of the family wrote to congratulate Duncan's mother, saying that when he was last in England Duncan complained that his life was a failure, with no niche for him at all. At the beginning of July Duncan wrote a detailed "Report on the Present State of Albania", which he sent to a friend in England, requesting him to pass it on to the Foreign Office. The message was that the only salvation for Albania as an independent state would be if the Great Powers sent "a well-organised little army, which would at first have to be composed of foreigners and be ready to strike in any direction at short notice". He did not mince his words about the quality of Albanian soldiers: "Without this army it is not possible to govern the country as the Albanians are savages and will understand nothing but force. Enlightened Albanians have pointed this out to the King time after time, even some time before he came to this country ...". He said that the present system of employing chieftains to raise armies was both ineffective and very expensive, since they claimed pay for double the number of men actually brought into the field. He concluded that "Should the King be able to put down the present rebellion without foreign assistance or a legion of foreigners, it will do him no good, as another rebellion will break out in every district where the tax-collector appears and we would again have no force with which to pacify the country."

In mid-July 1914, on his return to England after a month in Albania, it was Jack's turn to bathe in the limelight; most of the daily newspapers carried long accounts of his march from northern Albania with the chief of the Catholic Mirdite clan, Prenk Bid Doda, in order to oppose the Moslem rebels from behind Durazzo. For instance, the Daily Chronicle of 16 July described Jack as "a debonair, monocled young Englishman" who commanded Prenk's artillery, consisting of one Austrian mountain-gun: "'It was curious', said Mr Armstrong, 'how the gun was a sort of fetish to the Albanians. The rebels would never stand shell fire, while our own men would run to me for the gun on the slightest excuse. My eyeglass was an object of great interest to them. They believed it was essential to the working of the gun, and I did not dispel the illusion, but kept the glass in my eye whenever an Albanian was in sight'". Jack had a more important message for the press, similar to what Duncan had reported to the Foreign Office; he stated that "The King of Albania and his officers have, I think, made Durazzo quite secure against further attack, but the manner in which the Powers have left him unaided is shameful .... It is, I think, obvious that King William can do nothing without European troops, and a couple of thousand disciplined men would suffice to restore order in the whole country". Jack gave his services to King William without any payment, and he was rewarded with the fifth class of the Order of the Eagle of Albania. One of Duncan's many duties at court was secretary of this order of chivalry, which King William had instituted at the start of his reign; on 27 July 1914 he asked Harry Lamb to arrange that official recognition be given to the award by the British government:

"I have the honour to forward to you a full statement of the services rendered to the Albanian government by my brother. My brother was on a visit to me, when the government decided to send a gun to the Northern force under Prenk Bib Doda. As my brother was one of the few people here that understood the working of the gun, and had offered to make himself useful in any way he could, he was asked to take the gun North. This he did. He assisted in the bombardment of Ishmi and Malkuts and on both occasions directed the fire well. He trained 25 Mirdites to serve the gun etc and these

Mirdites worked the gun better than all the other volunteers in this country. My brother was away from Durazzo about a month and for part of the time lived on bread and water, sleeping in the open for three weeks. When Prenk Bib Doda's army fled in disorder, my brother saved the gun with all the ammunition and after great hardships got everything back safely to Durazzo. He did extraordinarily well all through and more than earned a decoration." (FO 320/4, fol 546).

Colonel George Fraser Phillips of the West Yorkshire Regiment (who commanded a small detachment of British troops in Scutari from September 1913) gave a more professional assessment of Jack's handling of the gun when he wrote to Harry Lamb: "I do wish you could have come with me to see (Prenk) Bib Doda's army; there were only about 2,000 left, and for the one cannon nobody can fire there is a Romanian prince, a French count and a young English barrister, none of whom have the faintest idea how to use it." (FO 320/4, fol 477).

Unfortunately for Duncan, he appears to have upset Edith Durham, whose caustic and forthright opinions about King William's court were regularly despatched to the Foreign Office in London. Although she was not lacking in a sense of humour, Duncan undoubtedly could not resist the temptation of teasing her, and his irreverent approach did not appeal to her:

Durazzo, Albania, 23 June 1914
"I had a talk yesterday with Heaton-Armstrong, the King's right hand man. A feeble stick with no ideas and the last man in the world for the job. We were on board the "Defence" lunching with the Admiral (Troubridge). Looking at the beautiful mountains I asked Armstrong if he were not longing to be able to get up country and explore them. He replied that he hated roughing it and hadn't the least wish to go anywhere that entailed discomfort. I said "What on earth did you come here for?" and he said "Because I'm paid". He maintained that he could see no fun whatever in camping or riding about – that he like good food and comfort. And he added that the day he had been to Tirana a dinner was prepared for the Royal party and that he had been expected to eat roast mutton. The Austrians as you know have a horror of mutton for some mysterious reason and this blighter is half Austrian. The next dinner he went, he said, he had refused to eat anything at all and he should make it a rule to do so in future. I told him it was insulting the people to behave like that – and

that he was quite the wrong man for the job. He replied he was doing it merely for pay and was not going to put himself out. He has never knocked about – he is merely a young chap spoilt by good living, more in place in a Vienna cafe than here. Who on earth appointed him?"
(FO 371 1896, fol 155-7)

Durazzo, 10 July 1914
"As for Wied and his surroundings, Heaton Armstrong 'the chocolate soldier' (a name which just hits him off), and the 'nervos' (von) Trotha, they do not even know how to behave ... I never saw a more pitiable show than Wied giving putty-medals to the wounded in the English hospital – as though he were feeding nuts to monkeys. Made no speech – looked bored to death and took no notice of either Dr Ward or the Chaplains or the German and Austrian ladies who had all worked hard and were grouped by the door.... The King has a nervous laugh which he fires off at most things. He asked me about some of my travels but has evidently not the vaguest comprehension of what life up-country means. I believe he imagines he is roughing it. The palace is very large and got up very swagger – butlers, cooks, all the paraphernalia. As the populace frequently points out the chief thing the King has done is to take their public garden."
(FO 371 1896, fol 195)

In July she wrote in the same vein to Aubrey Herbert :

"I have little or no sympathy with the King. He is a blighter. Why or by whom he was chosen is a mystery. Surely those responsible must have known he was a feeble stick, devoid of energy or tact or manners and wholly ignorant of the country? They are very Royal – both of them – keep a court and keep people standing in their presence. It is all ludicrous. The Queen, the few times I have spoken to her, impresses me as a bright young woman, but her only idea is to play Lady Bountiful, distribute flowers, put medals on the wounded and make fancy blouses of native embroidery. As for the King he seems a hopeless combine of pretentiousness and incapacity .... The King might have pulled through if he had a decent entourage. But Heaton-Armstrong is the wrongest man for his post that could have been found. His nickname of the chocolate soldier exactly hits him off. He tells everyone that he only came for the pay. He boasted to me that when he, together with all the Royal party, were invited to dinner at a Bey's house, he refused all the dishes. Said he'd sworn not to eat any of their food. I told him if he meant to succeed here he must eat everything and take a pill afterwards if necessary...." (Margaret FitzHerbert, The Man who was Greenmantle, page 126)

To Edith Durham, the world beyond Albania was full of "blighters" and "feeble sticks", and had her despatches to the Foreign Office been more balanced and temperate, she would have gained greater respect. As for Duncan, his gallantry is evident from his own memoirs and is well attested by other observers throughout May and June 1914. For instance, on 18 May he rode out alone to meet the rebels, and in the serious fighting on 15 June and the following days, he showed great energy and disregard for his own safety.

The last chapter of Duncan's memoirs describes his sad departure from Durazzo on 22 August 1914 to escort the royal children and ladies in waiting back to Queen Sophie's home at Waldenburg in Germany: "I had dreamed of remaining here and making a career and now it was rapidly disappearing in the dusk". Graver misfortunes befell Duncan in Germany, for he was arrested and detained as the first prisoner of war. It is frankly impossible to understand why King William never responded to Duncan's many urgent pleas, since a word from him would have ensured his release. William's later explanation, in 1937, that there was a fear that Duncan might return to Albania and "raise the northern clans" against the Austrians, was preposterous.

In the early months of the First World War, Duncan's younger sister, Bertha Grace Heaton-Armstrong, worked in the office of the Censor of Mails in the War Office in London. In January 1915, the head of the Censor office made accusations that she was pro-German. As a result of these reports, the Conservative MP for Hammersmith, Sir William Bull, asked a question in the House of Commons, as to whether the government was aware that in the Censor's office "there is employed a lady whose mother is a native of Austria, and her father half English and half Austrian, and whether he is aware that her brother is private secretary to an exalted person in Germany, and that he communicated with his sister expressing strong sympathies with Germany?". Fortunately the Postmaster General, Charles (later Sir Charles) Hobhouse, was able to put the record straight: Bertha was "the daughter of an ex-MP, who himself was the son of an Irish gentleman and an Austrian lady and married to an Austrian lady. Both ladies became in the ordinary course British subjects on marriage.". He then told how, despite being given a safe-conduct by King William to return to Germany, Duncan had been incarcerated. He added that Bertha's other brother, Jack, was now serving with the 20th Deccan Horse in France. The Under Secretary had seen some of Duncan's private correspondence, and "had found therein many expressions of his desire to return to his regiment and his country". He admitted that since the outbreak of war, Bertha had written to a relation in Germany "on domestic matters" and to enquire as to the whereabouts of her brother. He concluded by stating that he saw no objection to Bertha's continued employment in the Censor's office. The episode conveys the difficulties of families with German or Austrian blood in the intensely nationalist atmosphere of the First World War.

Meanwhile, Duncan spent two years as a prisoner of war before being released on exchange on July 1916. After a spell at the War Office in London, he was at last able to rejoin his old regiment in France in January 1917, but in an non-combatant roll as a pay-master. While on leave he met Thelma Eileen Scott, whose father was a politician and MP in Tasmania; she had come to work in England as a nurse. They married in December 1920 and went to live in Vienna. There were two children, Griselda Nonee, born in 1922, and Thomas Michael Robert, born in 1925. Duncan went into business with George von Trapp, a member of the musical family, but later moved to Slovakia, where he enjoyed limitless shooting. He remained in close touch with England, and served as a Gold Staff officer at the coronation of King George VI in 1937. During the 1930s he managed a large group of farms for his cousins in Austria, sharing the considerable profits with them. In 1938 when Hitler invaded the country, the family moved to Switzerland. In the following year, on the outbreak of war, they moved again to London, and for a period Duncan returned to work at the War Office in London, before moving to Herefordshire to run a prisoner of war camp for Italians. Thelma died in December 1967 and Duncan on 1 May 1969 at his house, Holymount, in Ledbury, aged 82. Duncan is remembered by his family as a kindly, foot-loose man, his main interest being in country sports.

Jack Heaton-Armstrong lost an eye in an accident as a boy, and hence his use of a monocle, which so impressed the Albanians in 1914, was no affectation. Despite his limited eye-sight, he served throughout the First World War in France, Egypt and Palestine with the Indian Army, rising to be a Captain. He was badly wounded; he lost a leg and was shot through the neck. After the war he did not resume his career as a barrister; he had a brief spell working in the Colonial Office, but joined the College of Arms, Queen Victoria Street, London. He was made an officer of College in 1922 as Rouge Dragon Pursuivant, and rose to be the second most senior herald, Clarenceux King of Arms, in 1956. He developed a particular interest in the heraldry of the RAF and its badges, and during the Second World War he was a reserve Squadron Leader in the RAF. In June 1919 he married a French widow, Suzanne Laura, daughter of Etienne Bechet de Balan, and the widow of John Whitehead, who had been killed flying in the First World War. They had one son and two daughters. Jack was made a Member of the Royal Victorian Order in 1937, and was knighted in 1953. He continued to work at the College of Arms until his death on 27 August 1967 aged 79.

The Significance of the Six Months Kingdom

Few people nowadays will ever have heard of King William of Albania; indeed there were probably many Albanians in 1914 who were unaware of their monarch's existence during his brief and troubled reign of exactly six months. It would therefore be easy to dismiss his reign as a footnote in the history of the Balkans, or to agree with Ismail Kemal's quip that "Wied is a void". Yet it would have needed a leader with the energies and abilities of King Henry V of England, or of William's ancestor, Frederick the Great of Prussia, to have created order and stability in Albania in 1914. As one contemporary Albanian commented "Prince William can only be criticised for being unable to perform miracles" (Fan Noli, quoted in Swire, Albania, the Rise of a Kingdom, page 195). I am conscious that Duncan Heaton-Armstrong's memoirs have little to do with the history of ordinary Albanians, and may be read as no more than an entertaining adventure of a well-to-do Englishman at a moment in history when it was possible for such men to follow their chivalrous imaginations without hindrance almost anywhere in the world, with effortless superiority. In her biography of Duncan's contemporary and enthusiast for Albania, Aubrey Herbert MP, Margaret FitzHerbert, states "Theirs was, briefly, an age of chivalry, soon to be laid to rest in the trenches of the Great War" (The Man Who was Greenmantle, page 117).

The story of William of Wied in Albania really belongs to nineteenth century rather than twentieth century history. During the course of the nineteenth century, the Great Powers had planted German dynasties in Greece, Roumania and Bulgaria, and these new royal families gave their countries a measure of stability, as well as connections with the leading royal families of Europe. It was a universally accepted truth that a newly created country would be in want of a prince from a respectable royal dynasty. Albania was now the last piece of the old Ottoman jig-saw to be given its own German dynasty, modelled on the royal courts of Christian Europe. After the First World War, it would have been unthinkable for the Great Powers (or the League of Nations) to have selected a foreign prince for a newly established nation; the process ran counter to the new principles of "self-determination" for small countries. During the first couple of months of William's reign, outwardly it seemed that the Albanians were immensely grateful to the Powers; the Albanian diplomat, linguist and eye-witness to the events of 1914, Constantine Chekrezi (1892-1959), summed up the mood on the king's arrival: "during that supreme moment of delirious happiness, the past, present and future misfortunes of the people and of the country were entirely lost sight of", and William was greeted as the "saviour of Albania" (Albania Past and Present, page 136).

The process of selecting Albania's monarch and placing him in the palace at Durazzo can be seen as one of the last minor triumphs of diplomatic co-operation between the six Great Powers before the Great War broke out. During the first three months of 1914, William was constantly re-assured that he was being sent to Albania with the full support of the Concert of Europe, and not just with the backing of those nations which had an interest in the establishment of Albania. Sir Edward Grey was insistent that all the Great Powers should act together in unison so that a neutral Albania could be seen clearly as the creation of an agreed European policy. This was, no doubt, reassuring to William and his advisors, and naively he trusted and believed the statesmen; indeed, in his memoirs, William returned again and again to the notion that his sovereignty was "guaranteed by the Great Powers". In particular, Germany and Britain found that they had a common policy with regard to the limited extent to which they would under-write, financially and militarily, King William's government.

Similarly, in 1912/3 it was easy enough for the Italians and

Austrians to agree on the necessity to create the state of Albania to prevent the Serbs, Montenegrins and Greeks from gaining complete control of the Dalmatian coast and the Adriatic. However, once Albania was a reality, their common interests ceased, and conflicts ensued. The Austrians were determined to preserve their access to the Adriatic since it was their only route for maritime trade into Europe; their fear was that the Adriatic would be turned into an Italian lake. On the other hand, the Italians regarded the Adriatic as their sphere of influence: "The two allies therefore fought, through military, naval and commercial missions, every inch of ground for local influence" (Gottlieb, Studies in Secret Diplomacy, page 158). The increasingly tense atmosphere in the palace in Durazzo among William of Wied's advisors and staff as the summer of 1914 progressed, mirrored the sharp deterioration in international relations in Europe at large. Up until about the middle of May, the King's Austrian and Italian advisors, together with the Dutch army officers, all worked together in relative harmony, but thereafter, it was a downward spiral as the Italians perceived that the Austrians and the Dutch were gaining the upper hand at the Albanian court.

The Italians interpreted the dismissal of their ally, Essad, as an insult, and thereafter there is good evidence that Italian agents were in close touch with, and even encouraged, the Moslem rebels who surrounded Durazzo. There can be no doubt that the Italians exploited the King's difficulties, although it is difficult to judge whether the overthrow of the Wied dynasty was their ultimate goal. When the British Admiral, Troubridge arrived on HMS "Defence" in Durazzo harbour in mid-June 1914, he had several long conversations with King William, who attributed all his difficulties to Italian intrigues: "What stands clearly out" Troubridge reported to the Admiralty in London, "is the universal impression that Italy is doing her utmost to compel the King to leave the country" (NA ref : ADM1 8386/210). Although we have no direct evidence, it is possible that the Italian royal prince and admiral, Prince Luigi, the Duke of Abruzzi (1873-1933), who visited Albania in April 1914, was hoping to replace William as King.

As the unity of Great Powers rapidly disintegrated, the strength of the Moslem rebellion in central Albania increased. The main demand of the rebels was that William be replaced by a Moslem prince. In selecting William to rule the country, the Great Powers failed to realise how different Albania was to its Balkan and east

European neighbours, and how inappropriate was their choice of sovereign. William had unwisely chosen his capital city on the doorstep of the most fanatical and "Ottomanised" community of Sunni Moslems, many of whom were descendants of refugees from Bosnia in 1878. The picture of these war-like Moslems facing the Christian prince chosen by Austria, symbolises the agony and difficulty the new nation was experiencing in deciding its true identity. Before they were ready to do so, Albanians were forced to decide whether they were to remain facing eastwards towards their Ottoman past, or whether they should embrace the less familiar Christian world of Europe. As the Ottoman Empire in the Balkans rapidly crumbled, the leaders of Albania were given too little time to decide. In this sense, the main theme of the reign of William of Wied was civil war. Unfortunately, neither William nor the Great Powers perceived the true nature of this struggle, and little was done to convince ordinary Albanians that their best chances for future development and stability lay in looking westwards towards Europe.

Aubrey Herbert compared William of Wied to the biblical David but without even a pebble or a sling with which to fight Goliath (Ben Kendim, page 162). He was in fact faced with several Goliaths, and in his memoirs he lists no less than 12 reasons why he failed to fulfil his mission as King. The first of these reasons was "the absence of a fighting force". Here we can perhaps identify William's greatest mistake as his failure, before he arrived in Albania, to insist upon an international force of, say, 3,000 troops, to accompany him in March 1914, in order to secure the Greek border and maintain internal security, for a period of perhaps five years. Had this demand been made as the foremost condition to accepting the throne, there was a good chance that the Great Powers, under pressure, would have agreed. It was, after all, no more than what the Great Powers had done in the previous century to secure the new German rulers in Greece and Bulgaria. Such a force might have deterred the Greeks from fermenting the uprising in southern Albania in April 1914; such a force would have denied Essad the chance of raising a Moslem army from central Albania, which then formed the corner-stone of the rebellion in favour of a Moslem prince.

William realised the necessity for such an international force too late. By the early summer of 1914, the Great Powers could not agree together to provide such a force, as they might have done in the early spring of that year; the political and diplomatic landscape had changed radically. By July 1914, Sir Edward Grey had washed his hands of the problem of Albania, and suggested to King William that he applied to Austria and Italy for support. In the end, not even Roumania was prepared to give William any military aid. The situation was entirely outside King William's control, just as on the diplomatic front, Albania's enemies, Greece and Turkey, were simultaneously being courted by both the Entente Cordial and the central powers in attempts to win them over as allies. In truth, he was ruthlessly abandoned by those who had enticed him to accept the Albanian throne. As the First World War approached, he was the helpless victim of the intrigues and quarrels between the Great Powers, and when the warships of the Powers pulled out of Durazzo harbour in the first days of August 1914, they even denied him and his young family the assurance they had given of their own personal safety.

It is easy to understand why modern Albanian historians have either ignored or ridiculed William of Wied and his court. If he is mentioned at all, it is to revile the Great Powers for burdening the Albanian people with such an ineffectual and inappropriate ruler. Understandably, the Albanians see the reign in terms of "imperialism"; an episode to illustrate how the arrogant western powers sought to impose an alien identity on their country. After the Great War, Zog borrowed, in an exaggerated form, many of the outward trappings of monarchy from William of Wied (who, in turn, had borrowed them from his former employer, Emperor William II); the brilliant white military uniforms, the orders of chivalry, the rituals of court life in newly built palaces and all the flamboyant paraphernalia of a "nouveau" dynasty. The comic opera atmosphere continued to appeal to the popular press in western Europe, just as it had during William of Wied's adventure. Yet all the while, for ordinary Albanians there were still no railways or decent roads, nor any real investment in education, industry or the country's natural resources. A generation of future leaders of Albania grew up hearing the rest of Europe laugh as the country attempted to gain stability and respectability through tinsel monarchies. It would, of course, be incorrect to attribute Albania's own peculiar brand of xenophobic Marxist-Leninism, which flourished between 1944 and the early 1990s, exclusively to the Ruritanian flavour of pre-war Albania. But is it any wonder that left-wing men, such as Enver Hoxha, felt revulsion towards such degenerate, pseudo-feudal forms of government? Once he gained power at the end of the Second World

War, he imposed a harsh Marxist dictatorship, ruthlessly isolating Albania from all but similar Stalinist, and later Maoist, countries. In this sense, William of Wied's brief reign may have carried a long-term and darkly concealed legacy.

Winchester, June 2004

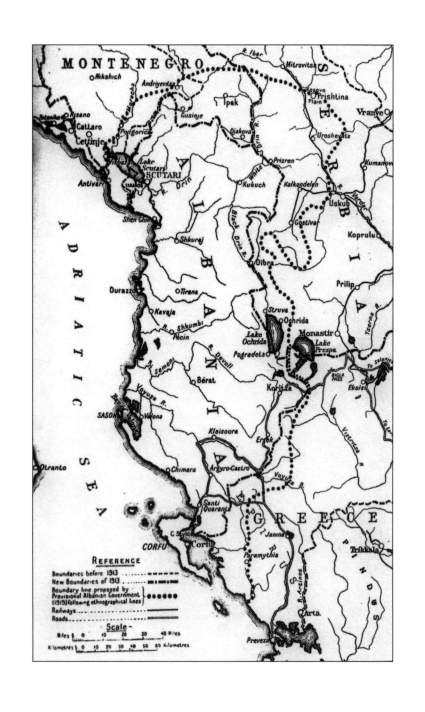

MONTENEGRO

Mkshich

Andriyevitsa
R. Ibar
Mitrovitsa
Kosovo Plain
Prishtina
Vranye

Ipek

Gusinje

Totonika Risano
Cattaro
Cetinje

Podgorica

Djakova R.
Drin R.
Prizren
White Drin
Kukuch
Kalkandelen
Uroshevats
Kumanov

Uskub
Vardar R.

Shkala Lake Scutari
SCUTARI

Antivari

Shen Chim

A
L
B
A
N
I
A

Drin R.

Gostiva
Koprulu

S
E
R
B
I
A

Shkuraj

Black Drin R.

Dibra

Prilip

Durazzo

Tirana

Kavaja

R. Shkumbi
Pecin

R. Devoll

R. Semeni

Bérat

Struva
Ochrida
Lake Ochrida
Pogradets

Monastir
Lake Prespa

Tserna R.

Koritza
BIGLA PASS
Eksisu
To Salonica

Voyusa R.
R. Vojusa
SASON
Volona
Valona

Ersok
Vovusa

Vistritsa R.

A
D
R
I
A
T
I
C

S
E
A

Kleisoura

Chimara

Otranto

Argyro-Castro

Santi Quaranta

C. Stylos
CORFU
Corfu

Paramythia

G
I
R
U
S

Janina

GREECE

P
I
N
D
U
S

Trikkala

R. Arachos

Arta

Preveza

REFERENCE

Boundaries before 1913 . . . .
New Boundaries of 1913 . . . .
Boundary line proposed by
Provisional Albanian Government ● ● ● ● ●
(1913) following ethnographical lines
Railways . . . .
Roads . . . .

Scale

Miles 5 0   10   20   30   40 Miles
Kilometres 0 10 20 30 40 50 60 Kilometres

The arrival of the new monarchs at Durazzo, 7th March 1914. Note the prominent position of Essad Pasha in uniform on Sophie's right

The Royal Palace, or Konak, Durazzo 1914

'Albania's New King Arrives: The Committee of Welcome' Cartoon
from the Literary Digest, March 14, 1914

"Welcome, Willie, I hope you find the palace comfortable."
Cartoon from the Literary Digest, March 14, 1914

The Throne Room, Royal Palace, Durazzo 1914

The Albanian Royal Family in the Palace Gardens, Durazzo

The Royal Family inspecting troops. Duncan Heaton-Armstrong is in uniform, 2nd on the left, between the two ladies-in-waiting

The funeral of Colonel Thomson, 16th June 1914, in Durazzo

William and Sophie in Durazzo, followed by Duncan Heaton-Armstrong

Baron Buchberger Captain Castoldi, Prince William of Wied, Durazzo

Prince William of Albania, August 1914

Turkhan Pasha Premeti, Prime Minister of Albania, 1914

Jock Heaton-Armstrong and Mirdite soldiers, 1914

Chapter One

. . . .

POTSDAM

How I, an Irishman, came to be mixed up in the Albanian adventure, really wants some explanation. I was shooting with a cousin in Prussia when the Albanian question became acute and read in the Daily Mail that Prince William of Wied had been chosen as the new ruler. Being what used to be known as a professional militiaman (a trade which had no future) I was on the look out for a more stable career and got in touch with Baron Esebeck, the Kaiser's Master of the Horse, who knew the Prince and kindly arranged a meeting for me at dinner. My original idea was to raise a bodyguard which could really be relied on. But the Prince turned down this offer as the Concert of Europe did not allow him to take on foreign soldiers. Just before the party broke up he came up to me and asked whether I would by any chance be interested in being taken on as the Secretary, should his negotiations with someone else break down. I told him I couldn't type or write shorthand, but would be only too glad to accept the job. When we parted he said he'd let me know in due course.

At the end of December 1913, I got a wire telling me I had been appointed Private Secretary and Comptroller of the Privy Purse and was to report at Potsdam within 48 hours, which I did. I owed my job to the fact that the Prince could not take on an Italian or a German for political reasons, and that it was a help to him to have found a 'neutral', who spoke German like a native and was a first class interpreter in French and Italian, in which languages most of the correspondence would have to be carried on. There were over 500 applicants for the post, in spite of the very low salary it carried. After the preliminary interviews, I began my duties as Secretary to the Prince of Wied at Potsdam on the 7 January 1914. It was a new experience for me to be in harness and it was not always pleasant, as never having been dependent on anybody I now had to behave respectfully to my new master, even out of office hours, which was not at all to my liking. However, my duties were light and I had nothing to complain about; in the mornings I had to report myself at the Prince's villa, to receive instructions for the day. As a rule, I only got a few unimportant letters to write, such as refusals to applicants asking for appointments, but sometimes I was sent into Berlin on all sorts of errands, some of which were quite amusing. Once, when visiting an official, who was staying at a well-known hotel in Berlin, I gave my visiting card to the hall-porter to take up to him. As soon as the porter saw my name, he handed me the newspaper, which he had been reading, and I found it to contain a paragraph about myself, which was anything but complimentary and much resented my appointment, as I was a British officer!

It is curious what a number of people there were who wanted appointments; men holding high positions in their own countries and ne'er-do-wells; there were Englishmen, Austrians, Germans and representatives from nearly every country in Europe. All their applications were immediately refused - but kept for further reference - hundreds of them!

Amongst the applicants for Court appointments there were some very funny specimens - adventurers, professional snobs and swindlers, and one had to keep awake when dealing with them. A curious case was that of a certain X.; his application had been refused twice, but he would not accept a refusal; after bothering me with his letters for weeks, he one day came to see me; for this great occasion he had put on a couple of decorations - perhaps this was done to impress me - I don't know! This visitor, who had a distinctly Semitic appearance, made a most unfavourable impression on me, so I got rid of him as quickly as possible. On returning to my hotel after lunch, the porter informed me that the man was still waiting and wanted to see me again; he advised me to have nothing to do with him, as he had met him twice before, using names and titles to which he had no right, and that he had on one occasion swindled my informant's employers, somewhere in the South of France. Naturally enough I took little further interest in this budding courtier and though he still wrote regularly that he would come to pay me his respects in Durazzo, I never had the pleasure of seeing him again.

We were much bothered by over-zealous journalists in search of copy, but as I was strictly forbidden to receive them and the Prince himself would have nothing to do with them, they had to go empty away. From the very beginning I warned the Prince that this was a bad policy on his part, but being of a very retiring nature, he would not believe that it is sometimes a most useful thing to have "a good Press" on one's side. During the whole of his short reign, the Prince only received very few journalists, and, as far as I remember, those few were English; however after a time I was able to get his permission to do so; but it was by that time too late and the international press had already turned against him, particularly the German press, which poured ridicule on the unhappy Mbret ("King" in Albanian) from a thousand scurrilous pens.

Occasionally I lunched or dined at the villa and on these occasions I made the acquaintance of several Albanian notables, among whom were Ekrem Bey Libohova, who later became Aide-de-camp, and Ekrem Bey Vlora whose undoubted abilities were unfortunately not made use of.[1] These two were Mahommedans, and "Beys", as the landed aristocracy are described; both of them are highly cultured and well educated patriots. They gave their future sovereign a lot of advice while they were at Potsdam, which advice was perhaps not sufficiently regarded; time and again they pointed out that the Prince could not possibly govern Albania without bringing an army with him, strong enough to deal with any league of Beys, or others, which might be formed against him. Unfortunately the Prince could not be convinced that an army was a sine qua non, though everybody else saw how necessary it would be! As already mentioned, I heard at a later date that the Concert of Europe had made the stipulation that the King would not be allowed any foreign mercenaries. I also made the acquaintance of the other members of the Court, who were being taken to Durazzo from Europe: von Trotha, the Comptroller of the Household, a typical Prussian officer of the best type, was as honourable and straightforward a fellow as one could wish to meet, and we were the best of friends during the whole of our time at Durazzo. Then there were two ladies-in-waiting, Fräulein von Oidtmann and Fräulein von Pfuel, the latter a sister-in-law of the German Chancellor, von Bethmann-Hollweg. Besides these there were the two members of a sort of Privy Council, who, though not actually belonging to the Court, were attached to it; these were Capitano Fortunato Castoldi and Vice-Consul Buchberger, who were to represent the interests of Italy and Austria respectively at the Court, though officially they were only the Mbret's advisers and political secretaries. Castoldi, being strongly recommended by his Government and as he was certainly a very clever man, soon managed to get the bit between his teeth and keep it there until about the middle of May, when Buchberger was for a short time in the ascendant.

At Potsdam the Prince worked very hard, much harder than I did at any rate, and spent the greater part of his days at his desk writing. Things appeared to remain at a standstill and nothing of importance happened; new arms, flags and uniforms were invented and it was my impression that too much valuable time was being wasted on such rather unimportant matters. However, I was very comfortable and did not bother my head about things that did not concern me; the Prince's amiable disposition made it a pleasure to do anything one could for him, though it was sometimes rather worrying not to get an answer on quite simple matters. His one great fault was that he could never make up his mind!

While I was at Potsdam, I met several of his brother-officers, amongst whom he was very popular, although they did not appear to have a high opinion of his qualifications as a ruler. During this time I made the acquaintance in Berlin of an Albanian lady and her husband, who had come over to Germany to see what was going to happen. One night I went to dine with this couple and was much amused by the very emancipated opinions expressed by the wife, who, though a "down-trodden" Mahommedan, seemed to have her husband well under her thumb.

Occasionally very disquieting rumours reached us from Albania, but eventually things appeared to have improved and von Trotha was sent down to Durazzo to make the necessary preparations for the King's arrival; he took the greater part of the European household staff with him and was kept hard at work trying to make the old Konak[2] more or less inhabitable. As may be imagined, he found things in an awful state! Nevertheless he succeeded in turning an Augean stable into a very respectable gentleman's residence; of course it was quite impossible to turn a Turkish Governor's Konak, which had been uninhabited for years, into a European Royal Palace. So time went on and after a period of about a month, we began our little "Lightning Tour" round the capitals of Europe.

Chapter Two

. . . .

VIENNA - LONDON - PARIS

On 6 February I received instructions to be in readiness to leave for Vienna, where I was to buy horses the next evening; I was kept hard at work till the time for leaving came and hardly had time to pack my luggage. I got to Vienna without any incidents and immediately set to work interviewing job-masters, horse-coopers and private owners; after a few days' looking and bargaining, I bought a very good team of bays at a low figure, so when the Prince followed me, he was quite satisfied with my work. He arrived in the early morning from Rome, where he had paid his first visit accompanied by Capitano Castoldi, who had been left in Italy, and Buchberger was now in attendance. At the station the Prince was received by an Aide-de-camp, whom the Emperor had sent to welcome him, a representative from the Austrian Foreign Office and a large crowd of people interested in the new country; amongst these was Dr. Gjergj Pekmezi,[3] a very cultured Albanian, and a number of Albanian boys who were being educated at some school near Vienna. These boys were the first people to cheer their future ruler with "Rroft Mbreti" (Hail the King!), which we heard so often after we got to Durazzo.

While the Prince was in Vienna we were the Emperor's guests and given rooms at the Hotel Imperial, where we were most comfortable; Royal carriages were put at our disposal and

altogether this first experience of public life has nothing but
the most pleasant recollections for me. Count Berchtold, the
Minister for Foreign Affairs, gave a dejeuner in honour of the
Prince; this was quite interesting as we here met some of the
men that had played the most prominent part in the making of
Albania. Only one topic was discussed - Albania and nearly
everybody present had something pleasant to say about the
country. Only one man in the room did not have such a high
opinion of her and that was an Admiral who had been there
himself.

In the evening we went to dine at Schönbrunn, the
imperial palace near Vienna, with the Emperor Francis Joseph;
this was a rather unusual experience for me and it must be
admitted that I suffered somewhat from stage-fright. We were
received by the Master of the Ceremonies and the Prince was
immediately taken to the Emperor's private room, while the
other guests, including myself, were assembled in a large
drawing-room; all the others were wearing their best clothes,
elegant uniforms with glittering rows of decorations, but I only
had a dress coat which did not fit me and had been borrowed
for the evening from a friend, as I had at the last moment made
the painful discovery that I had forgotten my own in Potsdam;
I did not therefore feel as comfortable as I might otherwise
have done. My discomfiture was complete when I was taken
out into the middle of the room, where I had to remain, stared
at by everybody, with only one person, the German
Ambassador, to talk to. The latter assisted the Prince to present
me to the Emperor, when he came in some minutes later.
Speaking German, the Emperor made a few very friendly
remarks to me; but in my agitation I addressed him as "Your
Highness", a faux-pas which his kindly good nature no doubt
overlooked. My neighbour at dinner was Prince Luli Esterhazy,
the officer of the guard, and we got on so well that we fixed up
a supper together that night and went on to the cabaret
Tabarin where I was recognised and given quite an ovation,
where we remained until the early hours of the morning. Next
day the Prince visited the Spanish Riding School at the

Hofburg, where he was received by the Master of the Horse, who showed us round and had some splendid horses put through their paces for his benefit.

That night we left for Berlin by train; an Imperial carriage had been put at our disposal and everything worked splendidly till we reached the German frontier, where I had to take tickets for twelve people in order to be able to retain our carriage; for the first time I was shown here that the Prince, like all prophets, was considered of little account in his own country! We took one day's rest in Berlin; I went over to Potsdam and completed my packing for the remainder of our tour and also for Albania and on the next we left for England. On arrival in London the Prince was met at the station by the King's Master of the Ceremonies and driven by him to the Ritz Hotel, where a suite of rooms had been reserved for him; after seeing to the luggage I followed with a secretary from the German Embassy. We were invited to lunch at Buckingham Palace, Lord Jack Hamilton receiving us at the door; my Prince lunched tête-à-tête with the royal family and I with the household. Hamilton, who knew me, said that everybody was rather disappointed when they saw me, as they had rather expected a bloodthirsty-looking bandit, who would have given them a break from the respectable routine of the court. When we left the Palace the Prince was in excellent spirits, and soon knew the reason when he handed me a red morocco case, which contained the Insignia of the G.C.V.O. (Grand Cross of the Royal Victorian Order)! I was green with envy, as I considered that I had deserved the decoration just as much as he had.

We left for Paris in the evening and got there in the early hours of the morning - too sleepy to take much intelligent interest in our surroundings. As the Prince was getting out of the railway carriage, there was a bright flash and loud report; I presumed that he had been blown up by some wandering anarchist and felt anything but comfortable; however to my great relief I discovered that the perpetrator of this supposed outrage was only an enterprising journalist, who had taken a flash-light picture of him for the morning papers. We put up at the Hotel du Rhin, where the Prince was known and had reserved accommodation. Later in the day the Prince went to lunch with the President of the Republic; I was not invited, which much annoyed me and injured my vanity, though it gave me the opportunity of doing some real secretarial work, to which I was already becoming quite unused. Our reception in Paris was distinctly poor; we did not get a carriage at our disposal and we even had to pay our own hotel bill; this last I did with a very bad grace, as the German owner of the establishment had stuck on his charges in the Prince's honour as if he had already been a crowned head. We left Paris the same evening and travelled through the night, getting to Neuwied, the Prince's ancestral home, in time for a late breakfast. We were put up by the Prince's two unmarried sisters[4] at Monrepos, a large modern country house, situated on the hill, overlooking the town of Neuwied and the Rhine valley.

I will conclude this chapter with a description of our visit to the Russian Court, though this did not take place till after the Prince had received the Albanian deputations, to which I shall refer later. On 25 February the Prince and I left for Berlin, en route to St. Petersburg. We reached Wirballen, the frontier station, at midday and were received by a Russian colonel, who showed us to the Imperial waiting room, where we had lunch, while he attended to our luggage and passports. The remainder of our journey we completed in a Royal saloon car, in which we were made most comfortable. In the evening we had a slight contretemps, which is worth narrating. Not being able to speak Russian, we were rather handicapped in ordering our dinner from the attendant, who spoke no other language; however we, by signs, made him understand that we were hungry and left the rest to his discretion; in due course he came to lay the table and at 8 o'clock dinner was served. We fell on the first course, which consisted of an ample Russian Zakuska, with a will, as we were very hungry and did not know whether we were likely to get anything else. Apparently the worthy waiter had received instructions to do us well and in consequence served us a long and excellently cooked dinner; not wishing to hurt his feelings, we ate of everything valiantly, and our glasses never being allowed to stand empty for a moment, we both got rather merry and delayed getting up (was it the falling of the hour, or drink that made our return to our sleeping compartments so adventurous?).

At St. Petersburg we were met by Count Totleben, one of the Czar's Aides-de-camp, who escorted the Prince to the Winter Palace. In the meantime, being surrounded by a crowd of gesticulating porters, whose language I did not understand, I failed to notice the Prince's departure and found myself left behind with the valet and luggage; I had no choice but to share the servant's carriage to a back door of the Palace, where the assembled footmen naturally enough took me for one of themselves; luckily a German-speaking butler appeared on the scene and took me to the breakfast room, where I found the Prince and joined him for breakfast. Very handsome suites of rooms were put at our disposal and also the Royal carriages. The Prince lunched with the Czar at Tsarskoe Selo and I was left behind to amuse myself as best I could and receive any callers who might appear during my master's absence. From my window I watched the troops changing guard and was much impressed by their appearance; the men were very fine specimens of humanity and in their winter great-coats looked enormous. The whole ceremony could hardly have been bettered, even by the Brigade of Guards, and the band was as good a one as I have ever heard anywhere. In the evening a dinner was given at the German Embassy in the Prince's honour, a very fine "Palais" with splendid hall and reception rooms; the Prince so enjoyed himself, that I thought he would never leave at all; this was rather an important matter for me, as I wanted to have a look round the town, which is famous for its gipsy orchestras. After midnight a move was made and after depositing the Prince at the Palace, Count Totleben and I were free to sally forth into the night. My host, an enormous man with a head like lion, could not have done more for me, but too much sweet champagne and unlimited caviar rather spoiled my evening and we went home rather earlier than planned.

It was noticeable that Totleben spoke German almost as his native tongue, but warned me that it was better to speak French when there were people about, as the Germans were so unpopular in Russia.

Next day we left St. Petersburg in the evening; at the station several ambassadors were assembled to see us off and a number of local Albanians also appeared on the scene; they forced their way into the Royal Waiting Room, while nobody was looking and, as they were unknown and unpleasant-looking individuals, I had them ejected without any further ado. We got to Waldenburg, the Schonburg's family place,[5] after an uneventful two days' journey and so our preliminary tour of the capitals was at an end; during this I had had my first taste of public life and I enjoyed every minute of it.

Chapter Three

. . . .

THE ALBANIAN DEPUTATION

The day after our return to Neuwied from Paris, the 21 February, was the great long-looked-for day, on which the throne of Albania was to be offered to Prince William of Wied by a deputation consisting of representatives from all parts of the country. The Albanians were to be received in state and great preparations were made for their arrival; everybody was arrayed in festive clothing and even I was made to conform to the barbarous continental custom of wearing dress clothes in the daytime; I did so under protest and even had my breakfast so attired. Ending a night in a tailcoat is one thing, starting the day in one is another!

I was then sent down to the station to await the arrival of the deputation; there were plenty of cars and carriages ready to take the Albanians to the Schloss and a curious crowd was assembled outside the station to give them an ovation as they drove by; so I had nothing to do but wait. On the platform I noticed another personage in dress-clothes, who later on turned out to be one of the Prince of Wied's officials,[6] sent on the same errand as myself; neither of us knew of the other's mission and when the Albanians arrived, we tried to elbow each other out of the field, each of us presuming the other to be some sort of impostor. When the train drew into the station, I soon spotted Castoldi's huge moustache - he was acting as bear-leader to the deputation - and he introduced me to Essad Pasha and the other notables. They were all wearing dress-clothes and there was nothing about them to distinguish them from ordinary Continental burghers; only their names sounded exotic and, as a German paper very aptly remarked, reminded one of patent soaps! Their appearance must have been a great disappointment to the crowd, who were expecting comic-opera brigands! I saw them all safely into the carriages and got into the last one myself; and discovered that its occupants were not deputies at all, but journalists, accompanying the party.

On arrival at the Schloss, the travellers were taken to a reception-room, where they were in due course presented to the Prince and Princess, who received them very graciously. Essad Pasha then made a very fine speech, which none of us understood, and when this had been translated by Ekrem Bey Vlora, the Prince made a short reply in French - or German, I forget which; this little ceremony over, everybody seemed very pleased and the Albanians cheered their new sovereign. So Prince William of Wied, a captain in the German army, became "by the Grace of the Powers and the will of the people" the "Mbret" (in Albanian)or King of Albania! The banquet which followed was not wildly exciting, as my neighbours were not very talkative and one of them showed his appreciation of the dishes placed before him rather more markedly than is usual in polite European society; however the wine was excellent and by the end of the meal, even the strict Mahommedan, Essad, had done justice to it. The Mbret, or King, as I will hereafter call Prince William of Wied (for to the Albanians he was King - not Prince, as is often erroneously supposed), then returned to Monrepos and we accompanied him; the Albanians followed us half an hour later and were entertained there for tea. A cinematograph performance was given for their benefit, but, though they pretended to enjoy it I know that it bored them just as much as it did the rest of us. During the performance I had to go back to the drawing-room for something or other; to my surprise I found it occupied by two persons I had not seen before; on discovering that they were journalists, I informed Baron Malchus, a person of authority in the Princesses' household, who gave the intruders a piece of his mind and drove them out of the house ignominiously.

Next evening we left Neuwied for Waldenburg in Saxony, Queen Sophia's old home; the town was gaily decorated and the population had turned out "en masse" to witness our departure. We started our travels badly, as Fräulein von Pfuel felt so ill that I had to dose her with brandy in the waiting-room while the King was inspecting the local veterans and fire-brigade; her condition did not improve during the night and when we reached Waldenburg next morning it was discovered that she was suffering from measles. Our new hosts, the Schönburg-Waldenburgs, the Queen's eldest brother and family, are one of the petty princely families which flourish in Germany and keep up a certain state, according to the traditions of a bygone day, though they do not own more land than an average Scottish laird. Prince Schönburg, who was killed during the first weeks of the Great War, was most amiable and, having seen British hospitality in our African colonies, where he had shot big game, did everything to make me feel at home under his roof.

The Albanian deputation reappeared here to pay its respects to the new Queen's family and the festivities bore much the same character that they had done at Neuwied. I quite made friends with the redoubtable Essad, though, as we could not understand each other in any language, our conversation had to be confined to slapping each others' backs. Essad Pasha makes a good impression on one; he is a square-built man of medium height with a high, intellectual forehead and piercing black eyes; his fifty years weigh lightly upon him and his jovial, soldierly manner inspires confidence. Essad Pasha was the head of the wealthy and influential family of the Toptanis and was by far the largest landowner in central Albania, where he could raise two or three thousand armed followers at a few hours' notice. It is rather a curious fact that most of his cousins were amongst his worst enemies and would not have anything to do with him. He was a general in the Turkish service and commanded the troops at Scutari, when it was besieged by the Serbians and Montenegrins during the Balkan war; his predecessor, Hassan Riza Bey, was murdered as he was leaving Essad Pasha's house after a dinner party and in Albania it is generally believed that one of Essad's followers, a certain Osman Bali,[7] committed the murder at his bidding. It was generally believed that the Serbians had sent secret emissaries to Hassan, offering £30,000 for the capitulation of Scutari and that Hassan, being a good man, had refused the bribe. Essad, with an eye on the main chance, is said to have accepted the money and surrendered "with drums beating and flags flying". What truth there is in the story, I am not in a position to judge.

Chapter Four

.   .   .   .

TRIESTE - DURAZZO

We, the King, the Queen, two ladies-in-waiting and I left
Waldenburg on the 4 March, accompanied by servants and a
few dogs; one of these bolted at the station and had to be
brought on to the next station by motor-car. We all wondered
what the future had in store for us; we had read as many books
as we could find about Albania, but it cannot be said that we
had any real knowledge of the country that we were going to,
and it seems that the King and Queen knew little more about
it than we did though they had spent months in preparing
themselves for their new duties. When meeting the King in the
corridor next morning, both of us dolled up in the newly-
invented, rather dressy, grey Albanian uniform for the first
time, I said "Good morning, Your Majesty", to which he
replied, "We'd better go a bit steady with the "Majesty" at
present." We arrived at Trieste at 9 o'clock. At the station we
were received by the Statthalter, Prince Hohenlohe, a number
of other government officials, local dignitaries, the officers
commanding our international naval escort and a crowd of
Albanian residents. As the King left the train, a military band
struck up a weird and rather cheerful tune, which we were told
was the Albanian national anthem, and to this we marched
solemnly along the platform, at the end of which the King
inspected a very smart guard of honour, furnished by the 97th

Infantry Regiment. The town was "en fete", houses were be-flagged and the crowd was in a state of delirious excitement - willing to enjoy every incident however petty. Our drive to the quay was a triumphal procession and I never heard more hearty cheering in my life. A motor-launch conveyed us over to the Taurus, a 1,200 ton yacht put at the King's disposal for this trip by the Austrian Admiralty; here several deputations were received before we again went on land to pay a complimentary visit to the Statthalter.

As his "Palais" was just opposite the quay, we went there on foot and a way was cleared for us through the crowd. However this closed in as soon as the King had passed, and it was as much as I could do to keep up with the procession; the crush was so awful that I got one of my spurs entangled in an old lady's skirt and had to part company with it for a time. I did not appreciate the humour of the situation and felt miserable at the idea of having to appear in this semi-clothed condition, so I was overcome with joy and gratitude when an Italian rough handed me my treasure, as I was about to enter Government House. I felt very flustered by this incident, so failed to get any pleasure out of the visit and was glad when we were once more safely installed on board.

Immediately after lunch the Comptroller of the Household, von Trotha, appeared on the scene, having just arrived from Durazzo whence he had come to meet us; he was not in the best of humours as the Court Doctor, Berghausen, had insisted on accompanying him. As Dr. Berghausen had not been expected, there was no room for him on the yacht and he was packed off to the French cruiser Bruix (one of our escort), where accommodation was found for him. Being of a very sensitive and nervous disposition, he considered that he had been publicly slighted and from this time onward was continually trying to pick quarrels with von Trotha, who very wisely ignored him as much as possible. We visited the Austrian flagship Tegethoff and our escorting cruisers early in the afternoon and the King and Queen were much impressed by the smartness of the Austrians and the cleanness of

everything on board; as also by the workmanlike appearance of
the British sailors on board HMS Gloucester, whose
commander, Captain Leatham[8] took charge of the escorting
squadron. In the evening we weighed anchor and,
accompanied by the strain of bands and the booming of guns,
steamed out of the harbour, surrounded by our escort - along
the Istrian coast - into a still Adriatic night.

Our journey lacked interest until we sighted the Albanian
coast on the morning of the 7th March, near the mouth of the
Boyana River; here the captain of the Gloucester won
everybody's heart by signalling over a message of
congratulation to the Mbret. The Austrian officers were an
excellent lot of fellows and, knowing the coast well, were able
to point out any places of interest to the new ruler (though they
did not know much about the shooting possibilities in these
parts, the only thing that I wanted to hear about).

San Giovanni di Medua, of which I had so often read in the
papers, the third port of Albania, turned out to be a mere
village consisting of half a dozen white-washed cottages. The
coast here is quite pretty and the sea was dotted with curious-
looking fishing-smacks, manned by Albanians, wearing the
baggy trousers peculiar to this district, who had come out to get
a first glimpse of their new sovereigns. Most of the morning we
spent on the bridge, the King smoking peacefully, the Queen
enthusiastic about every rock in this romantic country; the two
ladies remained below with the two advisers as the breeze was
stiffening and they were not particularly good sailors. At about
midday the wind dropped and by the time we got round the
cape and headed into the bay of Durazzo, the weather was
absolutely perfect, as was only right and proper on such an
auspicious occasion.

Durazzo was at that time a small town of roughly 7,000
inhabitants, a large number of whom were gipsies; it lies on the
southern extremity of a strip of land, which being cut off from
the mainland by the swamps, is practically a peninsula. White
houses nestling close under the hill, against a grey-green
background, is the first we saw of the capital; a beautiful bay

with a deep blue Southern sea and in the distant South, across the water, Tomor with its snow-capped peak, the Fujiyama of Albania. Little did we think when we looked at the town and its peaceful surroundings that before three months were out the Mbret would be forced to flee from it! The guns in the old Venetian fort boomed out their salute, as also did the warships lying in the harbour, and soon the busy little government motor-boat was bringing the great men of the land to welcome their sovereigns. (This motor-boat is said to have been one of Essad Pasha's "jobs"; it cost the Albanian government 36,000 crowns and was certainly not worth more than 2,000 at the outside.) Essad was of course one of the first to arrive on board and welcomed the Mbret in a few well-chosen words, in the name of the whole people; among his companions there were some distinctly strange-looking individuals, though they were, perhaps, all worthy and honourable men. Their oriental salaams and national headgear clashed with the frock coats and American boots that they were wearing. The Albanians are great on outward and visible signs; so to show their independence they discarded the old red Turkish fez and invested a new-shaped thing without a tassel, a reddish grey in colour, which was nothing like as smart as the older head-covering. Essad Pasha was even wearing dress-clothes, to show the King that one man at least in the country knew what was the correct thing to do! The King had had a General's uniform made for Essad in Potsdam, as he thought that this attention would gratify the redoubtable chieftain, and in this he was right; we had it handy and the Pasha came down to my cabin, where he immediately donned it. He seemed very pleased with his martial appearance and from that time onward always wore uniform.

The whole party was conveyed to the rickety landing-stage in launches; it was adorned with red carpets and bright bunting; and the native gendarmerie in their dark green uniforms lined the route that we were to take. The King and Queen walked at our head, escorted by Essad Pasha, then came von Trotha, the two ladies and I, while Castoldi and

Buchberger acted as rearguard; the market-square was crowded to overflowing and the people cheered, applauded and cried with joy! For five hundred years the Turk had ruled the country and now at last Albania had a Mbret - and what a one! No doubt the enthusiasm had been much augmented by stories, which had been circulated amongst the simple mountaineers, that a King would bring such prosperity into the country that even the poorest peasant would own his flock of sheep; others again had heard that bags full of Napoleons were going to be distributed amongst them and had come from their distant villages to be present at this interesting ceremony. The King's height and soldierly bearing made a great impression on the natives and no doubt many a crafty old brigand hoped that this tall young ruler would lead his Skipetars (Albanians) on some great sheep-stealing expeditions into Serbia and perhaps even conquer that country before the year was out!

What a mixture of peoples and costumes was assembled on the square to welcome us! Tall mountaineers from the north, with long narrow heads and fair hair, the shorter wiry Tosks from the South, whose sallow complexions and round heads proclaimed the Greek or Turkish strain in their blood, and lastly swarms of gipsies, many of them very dark skinned. Every district had sent its contingent to cheer the new rulers and their various national dresses added brightness to the scene. Flowers were strewn in our path and somebody in the crowd threw a couple of white pigeons in front of the Queen "for luck", as we were told. She picked them up and the people cheered themselves hoarse. A hundred yards or so brought us to the Royal garden, a very pretty little garden full of trees, which came right down to the seashore; the almond-trees were in blossom and their delicate perfume filled the air. Then we went up the steps of the Palace, a solid yellow house with green shutters, a cool stone-paved courtyard in the middle of it. However we had no time to examine our new home more closely as deputations and official personages had first to be received; everything seems jumbled up and I can only remember that Dutch officers, Commissioners of Control and foreign consuls were brought up for presentation to the King in endless succession, all in their best clothes and smothered in decorations.

At last our arduous duties accomplished to everybody's satisfaction, we were able to have our first look-round and start our inspection of the house; the first floor contained the living-rooms and on this were my quarters. As the house was rather small I only got one room, next to the King's study, and had to fix it up as bed-room and office combined; as it was triangular in shape, this was quite a simple matter and the view from my window compensated me for the lack of space. Certainly I was no worse off than anybody else, and as my room was very conveniently situated I had nothing to grumble about.

The King and Queen had sent all their furniture from Germany, some of which was beautifully inlaid old stuff, I believe of Dutch origin, so we were quite well off in this respect. On the first floor there was a "throne-room", as we called it, with a balcony overlooking the garden, and next to this was a drawing-room through which one reached the Queen's little boudoir. Then came a large, comfortable dining-room, with a very pretty view on to one of the old Venetian towers with the sea in the background; the other half of the floor was divided off from our part of the house and was occupied by the servants' quarters. The King's study was a snug room with big black book-cases and gun-cupboards round it; a large settee stood opposite the solid old work-table. As far as I recollect, there were few pictures on the walls, as these were reserved for the King's sporting trophies, which we intended putting up at a later date. There was a broad passage all round the inner side of the house, and in our half of it we divided this up with curtains, practically converting it into three additional living-rooms. The end one of these was furnished in the oriental style with sofas, cushions and rugs and was used as a sitting-room by the "entourage" when we were left to ourselves, as it was just outside the dining-room, it took the place of a lounge and in it black coffee was served after meals. The house was clean and, though not large enough for a Palace, was bright and comfortable. An excellent English butler, one of the old school, and his German footmen had worked hard to get the place ship-shape with the aid of numerous maids and 'dailies' of various nationalities.

When we sat down to dinner that first evening, everybody was in the best of spirits, as was only natural after the splendid reception that had been accorded to us. The enthusiasm of the population was indescribable and the King and Queen had to keep reappearing on the balcony to show themselves to their loyal subjects, who were cheering themselves hoarse in their honour. Chinese lanterns illuminated the square and an Italian brass band, which had been brought over from Bari for the festivities, played popular tunes, though it must be admitted that the music did not appear to have any charms for the native element. After dinner I went for a tour of exploration in the town and soon discovered the "Hotel" Clementi, the only European hotel in Durazzo, where the Dutch officers and a few other foreigners were celebrating the King's accession. This "Hotel" was anything but luxurious, though the prices asked were enormous. Simple fare was served at a long table, covered with a dirty table-cloth, and the guests sat round it on kitchen chairs and empty packing-cases; a couple of gaudy picture-postcards decorated the walls and an oil lamp illuminated the scene. To-night champagne was flowing freely, so I spent a pleasant half-hour with the soldiers, diplomats, soldiers of fortune and commercial travellers here assembled, all of whom gave me a hearty welcome. As nothing else of interest was to be discovered in the whole town, I soon returned to the palace, where I found everybody resting after our strenuous day; it had been a long and interesting day, this 7th of March, and as long as I live I shall not forget it! It opened up a new life to us all, a life of work and (we hoped) romantic adventure; Albania was a wilderness and we were all to take our part in turning it into a civilised country; would to God we had succeeded!

Chapter Five

. . . .

Small Beginnings

During the first few days at Durazzo the King and Queen were kept fully occupied receiving deputations from all parts of the country; as the court had no traditions, we were able to invent our own ceremonial, which we made as simple as possible. The King and Queen used to stand in the blue drawing-room (throne-room) attended by the two ladies-in-waiting, while von Trotha and I were kept busy looking after the visitors, whom we drove into the room and out of it, as occasion demanded. Most of these deputations were composed of feudal chieftains, or headmen of the towns and villages, supported by the spiritual representatives of their district - Mahommedans, Roman Catholics and Greek Orthodox. Occasionally some member of a deputation would be able to make his little speech in French or Italian, but as a rule the addresses and the general conversation had to be translated by one of the local dignitaries, who always attended these functions to act as interpreter. Some of the hardy mountaineers that came to pay homage were about as fine-looking specimens of semi-barbaric manhood as one could wish to see, and decked out in their best clothes made a very fine picture. Though unfortunately many of these patriots were not in the habit of squandering their fortunes on soap, and had strengthened themselves for this auspicious occasion with a mouthful of garlic, their manners were naturally graceful and their bows often as elegant as those of any courtier in Europe. Some of them were splendidly arrayed, their short jackets one mass of gold lace and embroidery. Around their necks they wore massive silver chains of quaint workmanship, to which in ordinary life revolvers were attached, but now were only ornamental, as revolvers were not allowed to be brought into the palace. Many a proud old brigand sported the medals that his forefathers had earned during the old Turkish regime.

Though most of these chieftains were entirely untouched by civilisation and some of them were certainly the most bloodthirsty-looking ruffians I had ever seen, they had a something in their bearing which stamped them as gentlemen. The most noteworthy of these chieftains was Isa Boletin (1864-1916), a native of Kosovo, in Serbian territory, who had spent the whole of his life fighting. For quarter of a century he headed one revolt after another against the Turks and finally, after the Balkan War, when his own district became a part of Serbia, he again found himself "agin the government" and retired to the small but independent part of his native land, where he made himself useful to Ismail Kemal Bey during the early days of Albanian liberty. The Turkish government had conferred upon him the rank of colonel, thus trying to flatter him into submission, but Boletin was above such peccadilloes and continued in the course that he had mapped out for himself. He was one of the first to welcome the Mbret on his arrival, and throughout his short and disturbed reign remained one of his most loyal supporters. Though a strict Mahommedan himself, he, like many of the Northern mountaineers, was very tolerant and placed his country's interests before his religion. Another interesting character was Dom Nikol Kachiori (1862-1917), a Roman Catholic priest of Durazzo and formerly Vice-President of Ismail Kemal's Provisional government in November 1912, who had done time under the Turks in various filthy prisons for carrying on his national propaganda under the very eyes of the authorities. As is to be expected, he welcomed the new monarch with open arms and gave him his wholehearted support; he became one of the leaders of the nationalist, or democratic, party and played an important role in the town, though his influence was not acknowledged in government circles.

When deputations were not being received, the King used to retire to his study for hours on end; Castoldi would be sent for and they would remain together till dinner, presumably discussing political questions. They were both reserved men and nobody knew what their plans for the future might be. There was much speculation as to what form of government would eventually be adopted: autocracy - oligarchy - democracy – any one of the three was possible, though for the immediate future autocratic rule seemed to promise the best results. The Nationalists, many of whom had lived abroad and made the acquaintance of liberal institutions, were unanimously in favour of having some sort of national assembly. Their most able champion was a certain Faik Bey Konitza,[9] a noble of the South, who had spent several years in England and America; he spoke English and French perfectly and was acknowledged to be one of the most highly educated men in the country. In spite of the aspersions cast upon his character by his many personal and political enemies, I believe that he was thoroughly loyal to the King. I know that he made himself very useful to me on several occasions, by bringing me information that might have proved most useful had it been acted upon by the authorities. He was, however, not taken seriously and his opinions were not consulted till all was already lost, and he then naturally enough declined to express them.

At last it leaked out that the King had invited Turkhan Pasha Premeti (died 1927), for many years Turkish ambassador in St. Petersburg, to form the first Albanian cabinet and on the 14th March this venerable old man arrived at Durazzo; a tall distinguished-looking figure, a narrow head, white hair and beard, a long aquiline nose and high intellectual forehead, these were the chief characteristics of this distinguished diplomat. A grand-seigneur in every thought and deed, he was however not the man to govern this turbulent little state, where deeds, not words, were wanted to weld the various warring factions into a united whole. Turkhan Pasha, though an Albanian by birth, had spent forty years of his life in the Turkish service; he had held important appointments in Crete, Asia Minor and in the Diplomatic Service. His long career showed a clean record for honesty, and this in an oriental official is a rare virtue in itself. He was generally respected and strongly recommended to the King, I believe by Roumanian official circles. Another thing in his favour was the fact that the great Essad had expressed his willingness to work under him, and this, too, was an important consideration. (As a matter of fact it seems probable that Essad knew more about Turkhan Pasha than the King did, and thought that it would be easy to influence him in the desired direction.)

After a few days' work the first cabinet was sworn in on the 18th March;[10] this ceremony took place in the King's study, as far as I remember, and I did not get the opportunity of watching it. This first ministry was composed as follows:

Turkhan Pasha Premeti - Prime Minister & Foreign Affairs; Essad Pasha Toptani - Interior & War; Aziz Pasha Vrioni - Agriculture & Commerce; Mufid Bey Libohova - Religion & Justice; Hasan Bey Prishtina - Post & Telegraphs (Public Works); Dr. Tourtoulis Bey - Education etc.; Dr. Adamidi Bey Frasheri - Finance.

The Nationalist party and many of the other amateur politicians of Durazzo were not at all satisfied with this cabinet. They objected to it firstly, because it consisted for the most part of "foreigners", men who had never resided in the country and knew little about it; secondly, because some of the ministers could not even speak their own language, and business had to be conducted in Turkish. Thirdly, it was thought that the Mahommedan Essad-party was too strongly represented. There certainly was some truth in all three objections: Turkhan Pasha, Mufid Bey, Hasan Bey, Dr. Michael Tourtoulis,[11] and Dr. Adamidi had for many years been non-residents. The two first-named had lived in Turkey, where Mufid was a well-known lawyer until the Young Turks came into power, when he had to retire from Constantinople; Hasan Bey's home was in the Serbian town of Prishtina. The two doctors had settled down in Egypt, in which country they are said to have had large medical practices. Essad and Aziz Pasha represented the landed gentry of central and southern Albania respectively and both were men of importance in their own districts. Although it is true Aziz belonged to the same class as Essad, and was also a Mahommedan, it would not be fair to call him an Essad-man; as landowners, they may have had certain views in common, but in most matters they did not agree and, as a matter of fact, Aziz Pasha was one of the greatest sufferers in the royal cause.

It was perfectly natural that these men should employ Turkish as the official language, as it was the language they had made their studies in and spoken all their lives. The Albanian language was not standardised until 1908 and had never been taught in the schools; it had been tolerated, but not encouraged by the Turkish authorities, who looked upon it as a barbarous dialect, wholly unintelligible to an educated person. I had several enquiries from Gaelic societies, who claimed that the roots of the Albanian language were of Celtic origin. Certain it is that all the ministers, with the exception of the two doctors, were Mahommedans, but they were westernised and quite liberal in their ideas. To begin with not one of them belonged to the Essad-party, though they soon fell under Essad's influence.

It was also intended that Prenk Bib Doda (1860-1920), the Prince or chieftain of the largest Catholic tribe in Albania, the Mirdites, should have been given a position in the cabinet; however this wily old chieftain would have nothing to do with it and, soon after the King's arrival, retired into his mountains in the north to wait and see what would happen next. One day he told Essad Pasha the following story, by way of an explanation of his conduct: "A fox and a cat one day made an alliance, as they hoped that their joint intellects would prove useful to both of them in their hunting expeditions; they set out together and met a pack of hounds, who invited them to join in with them. The cat, scenting danger, hastily climbed up a neighbouring tree, but the fox, being over-certain of his superior cunning, joined in with them. For a time they hunted together, apparently the best of friends; but one day the hounds, becoming tired of the tricky ways of their new companion, turned on him suddenly and tore him to shreds; the cat had never had any spoils of the chase, but it lived the longest!" Prenk, like the cat, thought that discretion was the better part of valour, and keeping out of Albanian politics saved him from all the work, as well as from the unpleasant experiences which Essad had to go through later on in the year.

The cabinet, once formed and sworn in, set to work with a will and started its glorious career by giving away all the best-paid appointments in the country to its political friends and, as the Nationalists maintained, to Essad's retainers. The ministers sometimes did not start their day's work till late in the afternoon, and used to sit together in Essad's house till after midnight, talking and drinking their coffee over innumerable cigarettes. They did not do any serious work and, in fact, I believe that they were incapable of doing any, though amongst them were some of the best-educated and influential men at the King's disposal. As one of the ministers once remarked "I cannot make out what the Nationalists have got against me; there is not a man in the country that can say anything bad about me - except that I cannot read or write!".

From the very beginning, the cabinet was unpopular and the mistrust shown towards it by the public probably damped any ardour it may or may not have possessed when it took office. Although Turkhan Pasha was nominally Prime Minister, Essad lorded it over everything and his so-called colleagues were afraid of him. The people soon got wind of this state of affairs and, rightly or wrongly, considered that Essad was only using the government to suit his own ends; Durazzo wanted the King to rule, autocratically if necessary, and they objected to Essad's "Tyranny".

Chapter Six

. . . .

LIFE AT DURAZZO

As soon as the cabinet had been formed the foreign ministers and other diplomatic agents began to arrive from all parts of Europe. The Roumanian Minister, Monsieur Burghele, was the first to be received as this avoided the difficulty which arose as to whether the Italian or Austrian representative should come first; not an important question, one would suppose, but at Durazzo a matter of supreme interest! As the Mbret's Aide-de-camp had at this time not yet appeared on the scene, I used to be sent in his stead to fetch the minister in a carriage (borrowed from Essad Pasha, as our own had not yet arrived from Germany) and an escort of mounted gendarmerie. On the first of these performances, I was mounted on a local pony; unfortunately for me it took it into its head to stop in the middle of the road, before we had reached our destination. Nothing would move it till some gipsies, who happened to be passing by, took pity on me and, making a determined attack, pushed me and my recalcitrant charger to the hotel by brute force. Here Monsieur Burghele was already awaiting me. Arrived at the palace, the minister and legation staff were conducted into the throne-room, where the Mbret, attended by Turkhan Pasha, received them. The Minister read out his credentials, or something, in French and everybody then assembled for lunch in the "yellow room"; the meal over, and coffee having been served in the oriental room, the diplomats were "processed" back to their hotel and, no doubt, all parties concerned were glad to get back into comfortable clothes. Monsieur Burghele's two subordinates were a Prince Michel Sturdza,[12] and Monsieur Ranette, both of whom were excellent fellows and later on played a more important role than is customary for such very junior members of the diplomatic service.

The Italian, Austrian and other diplomatic missions were received in a similar manner. The two former not only brought their large staff but also a whole bevy of officers from the ships, and others, just to show the people of Durazzo what great and powerful countries they represented. These two legations found fairly good accommodation in their respective consulates, which were amongst the largest and most comfortable houses in the town. The Italian minister came to Durazzo with the reputation of being a very astute diplomat; his name was Baron Aliotti and he had held positions in the embassies at Vienna, Paris and Washington. The Austrian, Herr von Löwenthal, was accompanied by his wife, and in their hospitable house I spent some of my pleasantest hours at Durazzo. On his staff was Baron Egon Bergen, an old friend of mine, who later became a member of Dr Dolfuss's cabinet in Austria.

During these earlier days, too, the King and Queen had to attend religious ceremonies held in their honour by the different communities represented in the town. Of these the Mahommedan, at which the Queen was not present, was by far the most impressive; the Mufti was so moved by the solemnity of the occasion, that his voice became quite shaky, as he spoke, and tears gathered in his eyes. He even honoured his own sovereign by praying the prayer usually only used for the Sultan - a compliment, which augured well for the future! The "Te Deum" in the Roman Catholic Church was quite an amusing event, as the aged Archbishop (perhaps he was only bishop, I don't remember) kept forgetting his cue and had to be kept up to the mark by his second in command, Dom Nikol Kachiori, who kept prompting him in an audible stage-whisper. This event almost ended badly, as to everybody's astonishment, the Austrian Minister had been allotted a place opposite the Court, right up by the altar, while the rest of the diplomatic corps were given places near the ministers in the nave. As soon as we got home, Baron Aliotti asked for an audience and I believe that he made serious representations on the subject. The Austrians claimed that because their Emperor was the protector of all the Roman Catholics on the Balkan Peninsula, they were entitled to this privilege. What was finally done to pacify the contending parties, I forget, but anyway everything was smoothed over more or less to everybody's satisfaction and a couple of days later the two rival ministers were seen walking down the street together arm in arm, as if nothing had ever happened to disturb their harmony. In this matter everybody's sympathies were entirely with the Italian Minister, which gave him a stronger position with the Court and Government than he would have had if the incident had never taken place.

At the end of the month the horses, nine in number, arrived from Austria; their landing was a matter of some difficulty, as the landing-stage was rickety and awkward for such an operation. A mare did succeed in falling into the sea, which so frightened her that a foal was found in her stall next morning. About this time, too, the Royal children, accompanied by Fräulein von Pfuel, arrived by the Italian yacht 'Misurata'[13] and were received in state. The Crown Prince, Carol Victor, known in Albania "Skanderbeg" after the country's fifteenth century national hero, was but one year old, but had a splendid reception from the populace, though he did not take any serious interest in what was going on; his sister, Princess Maria Eleanora, was a precocious child of four. Their stay in Durazzo cannot have been very pleasant for them, as they and their English nurse hardly ever left the little garden in front of the palace. The Princess, who married a Roumanian, disappeared after the Second World War and the family, having failed to get any news through the embassies in Bucharest, appealed to me for help. A friend of mine discovered that she had tried to escape from the country, had been caught and condemned to 18 years imprisonment.[14]

By now we had settled down more or less comfortably and our Court had been completed by the nomination of a chamberlain, Sami Bey Vrioni,[15] an Aide-de-camp, Major Ekrem Bey Libohova and an Orderly Officer, Selim Bey Wassa. Sami Bey, the son of Omar Pasha Vrioni (1839-1928), an influential and highly respected landowner of Fieri, was a cheerful little man of middle age and had sat in the Turkish parliament for his district, in which he is said to have been very popular. His figure having lost some of the charms of early youth, he used to dread the Queen's long walks over the hills, which he always alluded to as "le Sport" and altogether he was not keen on any form of exercise or work. Though the son-in-law of Essad Pasha, he did not take his part politically, but he always thought that his father-in-law, in spite of all his faults, was loyal to the King and doing his best for the country.

Ekrem Bey, whom as the reader will remember, I had already met in Berlin was educated in Belgian military schools, for a time under General Leman, the defender of Liége, and distinguished himself on the Turkish side during the Balkan War. Speaking French fluently, almost as his native language, and having a good working knowledge of German and Italian, in addition to Albanian, Turkish and a little Greek, he was a great acquisition to the international Court of Durazzo. He was good company, but very diplomatic, so that it was sometimes rather difficult to make out what he was really thinking. He was, perhaps, rather too nervous of hurting the King's feelings, always insisting that von Trotha and I should tell him all the unpleasant truths, but on the whole he gave the King good advice and was thoroughly loyal to him. Selim Bey, who started his career with six week's leave, belonged to a well-known Roman Catholic family of the North. He was a well-educated young fellow, speaking French, German and Italian fairly well; educated in Constantinople, he had mixed a lot with foreigners and was quite European in his outlook on life. He was the only one of the new trio who was always ready to give one a helping hand at one's work and, when I left, took over my office from me. A year or two later he died of tuberculosis.

Servants also we had in plenty and sufficient variety: Germans, Austrians, Albanians, British, Italian and an Egyptian Arab; nobody can accuse us of not having had a cosmopolitan household! In spite of the language and race difficulties, the Court got on very well with itself and we were just like a large family. As a general rule French and German were the languages most spoken at Court, but Italian, Turkish and Albanian had their innings when any more important function took place in the Palace. The "cuisine" and cellar were excellent; the cigars and cigarettes all that could be desired, so we rejoiced in all home comforts and the blessings of civilisation. The palace was an oasis in the desolation of the wilderness, so it is not to be wondered at that we were happy and contented with our lot! The climate was superb at this time of the year, just like that on the Riviera.

We used to start our day at 9 o'clock; breakfast was served in the dining-room, the King and Queen however having theirs in their own rooms upstairs. At 10 o'clock I started my ordinary secretarial duties, which kept me occupied till lunch. Often I was kept so busy seeing people that I hardly found time even to look through the morning's correspondence. At 2.30 I again retired to my room, where I usually remained till tea, which we had with the King and Queen in the passage-drawing-room. After this they, or one of them usually went for a walk and some of us were told off to accompany them; Sami Bey and one of the ladies-in-waiting usually accompanied the Queen. None of us appreciated this honourable duty, as the royal promenades were too stately to be amusing; a squad of gendarmes marched in front and one followed behind, while the Queen's dog, which was the bane of our existence, yapped all round one from the moment that the procession left the house till it returned to it. When I was off duty, I used to go for a good long walk over the hills, or have a gallop on the fields behind the town. Dinner was at 8 o'clock and after that we used to sit about till the King and Queen retired for the night; sometimes we played chess or cards and on rare occasions had

some music. The Queen played several string instruments well
and had a large repertoire of old songs, which she sang with
great taste to her own accompaniment. Herr von Trotha also
played the guitar and had a good stock of German songs with
rousing choruses, so our musical evenings were quite enjoyable.
After everybody had gone to bed, von Trotha and I used to
foregather in the oriental room to discuss the gossip of the day
over a bottle of wine, and often we sat together till the early
hours making plans for the future and criticising our betters.
This was practically the only really peaceful hour during the
day and we used to enjoy it!

Every week the King and Queen went for two or three rides
and I usually accompanied them with Ekrem Bey, as I enjoyed
the gallop along the sands, in spite of the two royal police-dogs,
who were in the habit of biting the horses' legs, whenever they
got the chance. On these occasions we were always escorted by
a detachment of mounted gendarmerie, whose equestrian
antics were quite amusing to watch. One day I was riding one
of the team that I had bought in Austria, a fine strong bay,
when he bolted with me, to the great merriment of the rest of
the party, who knew that I was no great horseman. They were
less amused, however, when I managed to turn him and rode
back into their midst, when I succeeded in pulling him up. The
King had a good seat and the Queen was an exceptionally fine
horsewoman; her little chestnut mare was a perfect devil and
nobody but the Queen could manage her.

So the first two months passed quickly enough;
occasionally there was some slight alteration in our
programme, but everything was apparently bright and peaceful,
though already in April signs were not wanting that this peace
would not last for ever. Early in the month the first reports of
the serious aspect of the Epirote rising reached us from the
South; the rebels were driving our ill-trained and badly-
equipped gendarmerie before them with the assistance, it was
said, of Greek regular troops and had already advanced as far as
Koritza, from where they had however again retired.

Chapter Seven

. . . .

APRIL

As was mentioned in the last chapter, the Epirote movement gained ground during the month of April and already in the early part of it news was received that the insurgents were advancing all along the line. As my work was at this time in no way connected with politics, I hardly knew what the Epirote movement was about, or what started it. However, it is certain that for some reason or other, the Southern Albanians, or part of them, wanted some sort of home-rule. At their head was a certain Zographos,[16] and they had the sympathies of Greece with them. The insurgents were Orthodox Christians and objected to having anything to do with the Mahommedans of central Albania or the Catholic mountaineers of the north. I also remember hearing that a compromise, a grant of some sort of autonomy, might have settled the whole thing in the early stages; however no compromise was ever arranged and instead of this the Mbret's forces were sent down to restore quiet. It seems certain that Greece did not respect our Southern boundary, which had been fixed and guaranteed for us by that great and glorious Concert of Europe, which has since so distinguished itself by its high ideal and humane culture. However this most benevolent of corporations was, as usual, divided against itself and this, of course, prevented it from upholding what it had itself established and guaranteed. In Durazzo horrible stories were told of the cruelties committed by the rebels; whether they were true or not, I do not know, but there was ample evidence to prove that they were at least founded on solid fact. Whole districts were said to have been laid waste and their inhabitants put to the sword, but I believe that this was much exaggerated. The Mahommedans, who had remained loyal to a man, were the greatest sufferers, but the Kutzo-Wallachs[17] were also persecuted and many of their priests murdered.

Prince Sturdza, of the Roumanian legation, was sent down to Northern Epirus to study the position and in due course sent in an official report, the nature of which I am unfortunately not at liberty to divulge. Von Trotha and I continually urged the Mbret to send home the ladies and lead his nation in person against the insurgents. However, our advice was not heeded and we remained peacefully at Durazzo, pretending that the Epirus question was not of supreme importance. Had the King taken the field at the head of his men, the Greeks would probably have been more careful about giving their support to the enemy; the King would have strengthened his position with his loyal subjects, and even had he failed and died in the attempt, all Albania would have respected his memory!

There were also plenty of signs of discontent nearer home than Epirus; the people of Durazzo were no longer enthusiastic and had given up cheering the King as he rode down the main street; people came to me daily with their tales of woe. The general opinion in the town was that Albania was being turned into a second Turkey; that none but Turks, or Mahommedans, could get government employment and that the King could never succeed in doing any good as long as the present ministry remained in office. Most of these grumblers were Nationalists, professional politicians more or less, or popular agitators who did not know what they wanted and were therefore chronically against all government, but I considered it my duty to report everything to the King, as I was well aware of the fact that his ministers and certain others of his entourage did not inform him of anything unpleasant that took place in Durazzo, or of what was the state of public opinion. Nothing ever happened, and that was very disheartening to those that were trying to help the King to make a success of the country!

As I could do nothing to mend matters and having plenty of spare time on my hands, I took up the plan of introducing sports and games into Albania. The idea for doing this was given me by a young Englishman, who having come to Durazzo for a few weeks on business, organised a race-meeting, which was an enormous success. He staked out a course on the sandy shore and the whole town turned out to watch the sport. The King was present and his subjects were delighted at seeing him in their midst. There were races for officers, European civilians, for town dwellers and for peasants, who came in from the surrounding villages, and the people of Durazzo were all delighted with this novel amusement. So I set to work to form a strong committee, consisting of Albanians and foreigners from the legations; our first object was to encourage athletic sports among the school children, hold meetings for them from time to time and later on to introduce games, such as football or hockey. Secondly we wanted to form a sporting club for the grown-ups, with golf, tennis and pigeon shooting and regular race-meetings at stated intervals. The scheme was well supported and the King encouraged it in every way possible, but the uncertainty of the political outlook and, later on, the actual outbreak of the central Albanian insurrection prevented us from doing anything to further the project. I believe that our scheme would have worked very well, had we only managed to start work in time, as the Albanians are quite a sporting people and would certainly have taken at least to pony racing. Good money prizes would have attracted the peasants from all over the country, and the people of the various districts would have got to know each other at the meetings.

On the 15th April a ship arrived, which had been chartered by the Austro-Albanian Committee (which was formed to foster friendly relations between the two countries)to bring a large deputation to Durazzo; this was headed by Prince Fritz Liechtenstein, whose brother was for many years Austrian military attaché in London, and Count Harrach; on the day of the Austrians' arrival they were received in audience by the Mbret. Next night they gave a great banquet on board, at which everybody of any importance in the town was invited; the two ladies-in-waiting, Ekrem and I were sent to represent the Court and most of the ministers were present. At dinner we had to listen to long and wearisome speeches relating to the old-established friendship between the two countries and the commerce, which it was hoped would now spring into existence.

Some days after this, one of our regular informants brought us a long story about a conspiracy to kill the Mbret, which, he said, had been discovered accidentally in an Egyptian cafe. It was believed to be of Young-Turkish origin and several Albanian Pashas were said to be implicated in it. As we never heard any more about this, there may not have been a word of truth in the whole story, but anyway it caused us quite a lot of excitement, which was at this time not unwelcome. It was also reported that the 'Black Hand'[18] had established a branch office at Scutari and was about to commence business on an extensive scale; Essad Pasha was to be one of its first victims and the other ministers were to follow him. As the society was said to be very loyal to the Throne and we were assured that the King was not in danger of sharing his ministers' fate, we took little further interest in its doings. In fact it caused us some amusement, as we told Sami Bey that his name was on the list and then sent him the inky impression of Selim Bey's hand in an envelope; the servant, according to our instructions, told him that a strange man, who spoke the Scutarin dialect, had left the letter and gone away, without waiting for an answer. At first Sami was taken in, but then he seems to have found out the perpetrator of the crime, as I received the same hand during the evening, with some threatening remarks added to it!

Towards the end of the month an Italian squadron, commanded by the Duke of the Abruzzi,[19] called at Durazzo; a dinner was given at the Palace and next day we went to lunch on board the flagship. The Duke made himself as popular with us as he was with his officers and in fact everybody he meets owing to his open, breezy manner. He took us round the ship the "Regina Elena", including his stateroom, in which several of his pin-up girls had been turned face to the wall, for fear of shocking the ladies.

Some days later we visited the picturesque little town of Kavaya, across the bay, and the Royal couple had a splendid reception from the inhabitants, who turned out in thousands to welcome them. A Mahommedan priest addressed the populace from a first floor window and from what he said one would have been led to believe that religious differences had ceased to exist in Albania; he said that he spoke in the name of his own community and in that of his Christian friends and fellow-townsmen and assured the King that the people of Kavaya would work together for their King and country like one large family. (Not quite a month after making this touching speech, our friend the priest was among the rebels, and all his loyal followers with him!) For this visit, the Durazzo-Kavaya road had been put into a more or less passable state of repair by Essad Pasha; two rickety bridges had been made safe for wheeled traffic and so we were able to drive the whole way in carriages. On our way home we had an impromptu picnic, which, as our European interiors were unable to face the food provided for us at Kavaya, was perhaps the most pleasant episode of the day. About this time, too, we visited Essad Pasha's political stronghold, Tirana, which had been proposed as the King's summer residence, or even as capital of Albania, but this expedition is worthy of a short chapter to itself.

Chapter Eight

. . . .

STATE VISIT TO TIRANA

On the 23rd April von Trotha and I, accompanied by the Dutch Major Lucas Roelfsema, who usually commanded the King's mounted escort, set out together towards Tirana with the coachmen and the horses which the King and Queen were to ride during their progress through the town. As we had a long ride before us, we started in the cool of the morning, at about 4 o'clock. Since this was a great occasion, we had to wear our tight tunics and astrakhan "Kalpaks", not the most suitable kit for a 42 kilometre ride on what turned out to be a very hot day. Our instructions were to halt outside the town and there await the arrival of the royal party, which was due at 11 o'clock; as the others were using motor-cars, it was of course quite on the cards that times would not be kept according to programme.

It was a fine, fresh morning when we set out and we had crossed the swamps and left the heights of Raspul behind us before the sun rose. Without incident we arrived at Shjak, a picturesque village some seven kilometres from Durazzo; we crossed over the river there by the high wooden bridge and rode through the narrow streets, which wore a festive appearance and were already crowded with spectators, and halted some miles beyond the town amidst beautiful surroundings. Here we spent a pleasant half-hour eating the breakfast, which we had brought in our saddle-bags, enjoying the lovely morning; the sun was already beginning to make itself felt and had in fact already begun to melt us, when we decided to make our halt. Then we rode on, the sun getting hotter and hotter with every mile; a "Kalpak" is a bad headdress to ride in during the warm weather and we cursed the man who had invented it.

At last, at about 10 o'clock, we saw the minarets of Tirana in front of us and, after half an hour's ride along the baking valley, came upon the gendarmerie detachment, which was awaiting the King's arrival outside the town and was surrounded by the usual crowd of children and sightseers. Here we dismounted and lay down under a tree, from where we could keep an eye on the road. We were rather stiff and absolutely parched after the last three hours on a dusty road; luckily for us an enterprising fruit-vendor had set up his stall near by, so we bought some oranges and lay in the shade sucking them, like Cockneys out for a holiday. We were much amused at the way that the King's reception was being engineered; a well-known Albanian politician and popular agitator, Dervish Hima, was holding forth to the populace which had collected on the road, telling them how to cheer, when to cheer and generally how to behave at the King's arrival. He waved his arms and shouted "Rroft!" time after time, getting the people to imitate him; when he considered that his audience was more or less word-perfect, and had held a final dress-rehearsal, he joined us under our tree and rested from his labours.

Our betters were due to arrive at 11 o'clock in three motor-cars; however the hour passed and nothing happened. At half past we began to wonder why they were so late and at twelve our wonder turned to anxiety, particularly as we knew that there were several very dilapidated wooden bridges on the way, any one of which might have been the cause of a disaster. We were much relieved to hear a tooting in the distance half an hour later and to see two cars coming slowly towards us along the road. In due course they pulled up by us and discharged their passengers; to our great astonishment the King's car not only contained the members of his suite, but also Essad Pasha, the worthy war-minister, who stepped out of the car all wreathed in smiles. I must explain how the last-named came to get a seat in the royal car, as this will show the reader more clearly than anything else what manner of man Essad was. On this occasion he certainly proved himself to be an "arrangeur" of the first order. Essad Pasha was originally to have shared a third car with Turkhan Pasha, who, as Prime Minister, would of course have played an important part in the Tirana proceedings and taken precedence of his powerful colleague. As may be imagined, this would not have suited Essad's book at all, as he was always very jealous of his position, most of all in his own part of the country. Therefore, in order to appear before his supporters as the King's right hand man, some "coup" had to be devised to keep his rival out of the way during the state entry. Together they saw the royal cars off and when these had left, Essad's was brought out of its garage; on reaching the gate, something is supposed to have gone wrong with the engine and the chauffeur disappeared under the car to look for the cause of the trouble. While all this was going on and the unsuspecting Turkhan was quietly watching the performance, Essad managed to slip away and jumping into a two-horsed carriage, which "happened" to be standing round the corner, drove off at a gallop in pursuit of the royal cars, leaving the unfortunate Prime Minister to look after himself as best he could! Essad caught up the King almost half way to Tirana - his horses half dead, but his object attained!

When he rode through the town, he did so immediately behind his sovereign - the one and only Essad Pasha - and the Prime Minister was altogether out of it! (That poor old gentleman followed us in due course and joined us after lunch, when his presence was no longer resented.) Tirana is a picturesque little town, half as big again as Durazzo; it lies in a fertile valley and is surrounded by hills, with high mountains in the East. To-day it wore a festive appearance and was full to overflowing, as the peasants of the surrounding districts had come in their thousands to welcome the Mbret (or had they come to do homage to their feudal superior, King Essad?). On all sides were detachments of "Militia", i.e. Essad's armed followers, who pretended to keep order in the streets. This militia, which consisted practically entirely of Essad's tenants, with a sprinkling of retired brigands from the mountains, was sent down to the Epirus some days afterwards, but did not show any particularly martial ardour, and it is safe to say that none of our other allies behaved themselves more discreditably. We rode slowly through the crowded streets, being stopped every few yards by deputations who made speeches and presented addresses of welcome; the crowds appeared most enthusiastic and an old-fashioned cannon boomed out a most impressive salute (one shot every ten minutes, as it could not be reloaded more quickly!). Tirana is almost entirely Mahommedan and one saw hardly any women that were not veiled up to the eyes; the sight of the unveiled Queen must have surprised and shocked the highly correct and religious community of the town! With all the pomp and dignity of Royalty, we wended our way majestically through the crowded streets and up a private road to Essad Pasha's villa, which stands on a hill overlooking the town; here we dismounted and after being regaled with light refreshment, sat down to lunch. What a lunch it was! Words cannot describe the horrible appearance and taste of the dishes, which were served in quick succession by servants who did not look too clean; soup, meat and pudding all tasted of mutton fat and all other imaginable nastiness. The Queen managed to swallow some of the horrible mixtures set before her and had the good taste to praise them, but the rest of us were taking no risks and stuck to the coarse, tasteless bread and mineral water. The annoying thing about it was that the natives were visibly appreciating the meal, though in deference to the European element they did not smack their lips and otherwise express their satisfaction, as is customary in Albania and other oriental countries. The black coffee after lunch was an unmixed blessing as we were all of us pretty hungry.

After this a general move was made to the school-house in

the town, where the next two hours were spent in receiving further deputations from the surrounding districts and bodies of Tirana worthies. On our way from the villa to the school-house I witnessed a rather uncommon accident; as we were riding along, I suddenly heard a piercing shriek just in front of us and saw a child in the act of falling out of a first-floor window. The child landed on the heads of a group of spectators, who were also frightened out of their wits; however as if by a miracle nobody was injured and the chief victim of the accident was led away by her mother in a flood of tears.

For tea we adjourned to Abdi Bey Toptani's house,[20] which was run on more European lines. Our host, one of the most respected men in the country, did not sit down at table with his guests, and according to Albanian custom, waited on us in person, taking the role of butler till the meal was over. Abdi Bey was not on the best of terms with his cousin Essad, though they were not openly at war with each other, and therefore kept out of politics altogether till after his kinsman's fall, when he was, much against his will, called upon to take a place in the new cabinet. At 5 o'clock von Trotha and I were able to set out on our homeward journey; Major Roelfsema joined us outside and together we left the town along the white, dusty road, which led to Durazzo. At first the exercise was quite pleasant, but gradually our progress became slower and slower; night came on and we had to keep the horses at a walking pace, as they were tired and stumbled over every loose stone on the road. We reached Durazzo at 11.30, half dead with hunger and fatigue; the horses were thoroughly done up and poor Roelfsema had to tramp the last few miles, dragging along his pony behind him. It had been a long day for us; 84 kilometres in the saddle, a broiling sun, much standing about during the ceremonies in Tirana and practically nothing to eat since our breakfast by the roadside; so we had every right to feel tired! We found the ladies staying up to welcome us and were more than grateful to them for the supper they had arranged for us; we ate everything that came within our reach and, after a gossip in the Oriental Room, over a last cigarette and glass of wine, we stumbled off to bed and a ten hours' sleep.

The Tirana expedition was voted a great success and none of us thought that exactly a month afterwards an insurrection would drive the King out of his capital!

Chapter Nine

THE OUTBREAK OF REBELLION

It was now May and the state of Epirus had been going steadily from bad to worse since the day of the Mbret's arrival, so something serious had to be done to regain the affected districts for the Albanian Crown. The Great Powers, who had so generously fixed and guaranteed our frontiers, did not consider it part of their duty or business to protect them; so they left this difficult task to their unfortunate dupe, the Mbret "by the Grace of the European Concert". The royal forces in the South consisted of some 2,500 gendarmes under Dutch and native officers and several thousand loyal Southerners, whose local leaders were supposed to cooperate with the regular forces. Attached to these irregular bands were a Captain Ghilardi (late of the Austrian Army)[21] and an American,[22] both of whom did excellent work later on in the year with a mixed detachment of native and Bulgarian "Komitadjis" (an outlaw or brigand).

The Royal forces had put up a good fight but could no longer hold their own against the Epirotes, whose troops were not only superior in numbers to our own, but also better equipped and organised by Greek officers, besides which they had a certain number of fairly modern field guns at their disposal. In Durazzo it was openly said that the Greek army was assisting the Epirotes and that this was the reason that they were so successful in driving us out of their country. Whether this was true or not, I don't know, but it is certain that the Epirote movement was engineered from Greece and received more than moral support from the Greek Government. Many of the insurgents killed or taken prisoner were wearing Greek uniforms, minus the distinctive badges in most cases, and the guns are also reported to have been of Greek origin. Anyway, to make a long story short, our forces had to fall back, and fighting almost continually, were gradually forced north by the enemy.

The King and Council of Ministers had many a serious debate upon this subject. Colonel Thomson,[23] the second in command of the Gendarmerie Mission, was of the opinion that the only way of getting back the Epirus was by diplomacy. As he had a shrewd suspicion that we were up against something stronger than we could tackle with our small and ill-equipped forces, he even went so far in backing his opinion that he attempted to start negotiations on his own, when he was Commandant of the Southern armies. The ministers and advisers were of course indignant at this and Thomson was recalled to Durazzo to explain his conduct. Essad Pasha, as Minister for War, was opposed to any compromise with the insurgents and assured the Mbret that the rebellion could easily be put down by force of arms; he carried the cabinet with him and it was decided to set to work in earnest!

The Government had purchased several thousand modern military rifles in Italy, machine and mountain guns in Austria and now thought itself strong enough to conquer the greater part of the world. The Mahommedan population of central Albania was to be armed and with this imposing new army behind him, Essad Pasha hoped to sweep all before him; at least he said that he would. Although Essad had been a general in the Turkish army and ought to have known at least something about soldiering, it never seems to have struck him that it would be a good thing to put some sort of discipline into these untrained hordes before starting out on his expedition. Essad's position was becoming very unpleasant, as owing to his murky

past, everybody's hand was against him and everything he did
was doomed to failure owing to the active or passive resistance
of his enemies. Most astounding stories of his disloyalty and
double-dealing were whispered in the bazaars and cafes, from
where they were brought to the palace. Everything was done to
collect evidence to prove his dishonesty, but as far as I know no
really damning evidence could be found against him, though
everybody felt convinced that he was guilty. In this the Italians
must be excepted as they, to then end, believed Essad to have
been the victim of an Austrian conspiracy.

On the 8th of May he tendered his resignation on the
ground that his personal enemies made all government
impossible, while he remained in the cabinet. He told the King
that he knew all the stories that had been circulated about him
and that there was not a word of truth in any of them. He
offered to go abroad and to remain in America for three or four
years, to show the King his honest intentions, and added that
he had given the King his word to serve him loyally and that if
he had a thousand souls, they would all be at his sovereign's
disposal. At this interview Captain Castoldi was, I believe,
present and acted as interpreter. For some reason unknown, the
Mbret refused to accept the Minister's resignation and coaxed
and flattered him into retaining the office, which he was
willing to give up and everybody considered him unfitted for. I
have never understood why the King did not jump at this
opportunity of ridding himself of Essad, without offending the
great man. Considering the way he treated him only ten days
later, the King cannot have had any great liking for him!

So Essad remained at his post and the central Albanians
were armed. Long caravans of ponies left Durazzo for the
interior, laden with rifles and enormous quantities of
ammunition. Hardly had the arms and stores been distributed,
when rumours reached us that the very people we had armed
had unanimously refused to march South, or in fact have
anything at all to do with the whole expedition against the
Epirotes, "as they did not wish to kill their brothers!". Essad
Pasha sallied forth to visit the affected districts - Shjak, Tirana,

Kavaya, etc - and after a few days returned to headquarters. He reported that the movement was not serious and had been caused by the tactlessness of some minor officials and assured the King that he had put everything in order, so that the people were now willing to march.

As Essad, whatever else he may have been, was an uncommonly clever man, he must have seen and heard enough during his tour to show him what was happening in the country, so it can only be presumed that he deliberately made a false report to his royal master, for some reasons of his own. In spite of his assurances that all was well, most disquieting news kept coming in from the surrounding villages; on the 17th of May the King received an urgent message from Shjak (only about seven kilometres from Durazzo), asking for strong reinforcements, as the town was surrounded by insurgents and could not hold out if attacked. As Shjak was at this time garrisoned by about 200 "Royal" men from Kruja, one of Essad Pasha's strongholds, the telegram was not taken too seriously and in spite of long discussions, nothing happened that night and Shjak was left to look after itself as best it could.

Among our numerous informants there was one who insisted that the Epirus expedition had nothing whatsoever to do with the rebellion, but that this was due entirely to agrarian causes. He told us that he knew for a fact that the peasants had only awaited such an opportunity to throw off the yoke of their oppressors, the beys, who owned the land and that they wanted to get rid of "Essad's tyrannical government". As I was all along certain that the Mbret was not being kept properly "au courant" by his ministers, who, through ignorance of the real state of affairs or some treasonable purposes of their own, continued to paint the situation in a rosy hue, I worried him, till he gave me his sanction to ride over to the insurgents next day, to have a look at them and, if possible, to find out what the trouble was about. Officially he had nothing to do with my expedition, as he did not want to take any responsibility and there was of course a chance of my getting into trouble. He could not be sure that I would not commit some "faux pas", which, if I went officially, might have caused the government endless complications. So it was decided that I should go in plain clothes; nobody was told of my intentions, as gossip was the curse of Durazzo and it is always well to hold one's tongue, till an experiment has succeeded.

Chapter Ten

· · · ·

A DAY WITH THE INSURGENTS

It was about 7 o'clock on the morning of the 18th May, when I set out on my little native pony to have a look at the insurgents; the King and Queen had ridden out just before me and I followed behind their escort, to make certain arrangements with von Trotha, in case of accidents. Outside the town we separated, the royal cavalcade keeping to the right, close to the seashore, whilst I continued on the Tirana road. As I jogged along, I wondered what was going to come of this expedition and felt elated at getting the chance of doing something out of the common. As a precaution I had taken an automatic pistol with me and, though I did not intend using it, whatever might happen, it gave me a wonderful feeling of safety and self-confidence. (It must not be supposed that any noble motives urged me not to make use of my pistol; the truth is that I had never fired a shot out of it and therefore did not wish anybody to see my lack of skill.)

The first stretch of the road leads across the Durazzo swamps, which are fairly dry round here and overgrown with high, thick scrub; then come the heights of Raspul and once these are passed, the road again follows a valley, the greater part of which is under cultivation. I kept my eyes open on the way, expecting some signs of warlike activity, but everything appeared to be perfectly peaceful and the peasants were at work in their fields as usual. At Shjak I found a strong gendarmerie detachment guarding the bridge over the river. The village was full of armed men, the Kruja contingent, and the oriental street life was going on as if there were no enemy within a hundred miles of the place; however I noticed that the people appeared to be very much surprised at the arrival of a solitary European. At the Governor's house I found that eminently respectable official, the officer in charge of the gendarmerie detachment and some of the village notables, lounging out of a first floor window. They could not understand how I had got through the rebels' lines and I found it difficult to convince them that the road to Durazzo was clear of insurgents and that the country people I had met, were not even armed. A man, who spoke Italian, acted as interpreter and through him the "Kaimakam" advised me to turn back before it was too late; under no circumstances was I to go any further, as "our scouts had seen a strong rebel detachment on the main road, not ten minutes walk from where we stood" and I would certainly be killed, or at least taken prisoner.

As it was evident that the worthies of Shjak were in a ridiculous state of panic and their information had so far proved to be wrong, I did not take their warnings too seriously and rode on. Somehow I felt that I would be as safe amongst the rebels as amongst our own people in Durazzo. At the end of ten minutes there was still no sign of any insurgents; the road from here onward serpentines up a long hill and on the top of this, some four kilometres from the village, I made a halt and had a look at the fertile valley on the other side of it. Through my field-glasses I soon spotted a strong detachment on the road, some two kilometres off; it consisted of about 2,000 men, most of whom were sitting about on the grass smoking, while about two companies were drawn up in line and appeared to be awaiting an order to move off.

As I did not appreciate the idea of riding into the midst of them without invitation and could not make up my mind as to what I was to do next, I just sat down by the side of the road and waited to see what they were going to undertake. I had not been here more than quarter of an hour, when two unarmed peasants emerged from a side-path. I stopped and questioned them as to whether they had seen any Komitadjis about. They looked at me suspiciously and did not answer my question but enquired first as to my nationality: was I Austrian or Serbian? I explained to them that I was British and this seemed to please them; the men's faces brightened up and their manner became friendly.[24] They now volunteered to personally conduct me to the nearest Komitadjis, who they said were very worthy men and friends of theirs.

On reaching a hollow, about a hundred yards from the road, we came on the enemy's first picket; a sentry was posted behind a hedge on the sky-line to watch the Durazzo road, which could be seen nearly all the way, and his comrades were lying about on the grass. They did not stand up to receive me and were a murderous-looking lot of ruffians, all armed with modern rifles, large knives or bayonets and revolvers of various, mostly obsolete, patterns. Though their manner was not cordial and their appearance altogether against them, they answered my "Ngat jeta" ("Long life", the usual Albanian greeting) quite civilly, so I dismounted, gave the pony to a boy to hold and sat down with them in the shade. My knowledge of the Albanian language is very limited, so we found some difficulty in understanding each other; this difficulty was bound to crop up, but I had not brought an interpreter with me, as I had by that time already discovered that the Albanians are even more suspicious of their own countrymen than they are of foreigners, and the presence of an interpreter might have spoiled my chances of hearing anything interesting. It must be admitted that our conversation was not at all brilliant and had to be limited to simple questions and answers, but I understood quite enough to make me feel certain that these rebels were no army of Essad Pasha's. In fact many of them appeared to be out for his blood, as "they wanted to do away with him and all other landlords, whose sole occupation was that of taking the peasants' money and then beating them!". Of course they unanimously condemned the ministry, which consisted of their old oppressors and did nothing to protect the peasant interests. From what they said, it was also evident that their religious fanaticism had been worked up as they kept on repeating "Mahommedans are good", "Turks are good", "Imams are good" and suchlike. I also understood them to complain that the schoolmasters were being paid higher salaries than the priests. As we later heard that this was one of the insurgents' grievances, it seems probable that I understood right. One man considered Serbia the best country, but this appeared to be his private view and was not supported by his comrades. I told them who I was and that the King wanted to see his subjects contented and happy; to my great surprise they did not disagree with this at all and several of them murmured "Rroft Mbreti" fervently. From this first picket, I was moved on to another and then to a third and everywhere I was quite well received. I told the men of the large forces and artillery at Durazzo and pointed out the masts of some ships in the harbour, which could just be seen through my field-glasses, assuring them that they belonged to Italian men o' war. As a matter of fact the Italian destroyer flotilla had put to sea in the early morning and had to be requested to return, by a wireless message, later on in the day. Although I knew this quite well, I thought it advisable to let the insurgents think that we were well prepared for any emergencies. We got on quite well with each other and my new friends gave me some of their bread and cheese, both of them the nastiest of their kind that I have ever tasted, and rolled cigarettes for me, which they shoved into my mouth and lit. I accepted everything that they chose to offer me and pretended to be enjoying myself thoroughly, though when I went away from the group for a moment I noticed that an armed man remained close by me all the time, which made me feel a little uncomfortable.

We arranged that a letter was to be written, which I was to take back to the King, and a man was despatched to the main body to find a scribe as none of the outpost company could write. While the man was away, I kept my eyes open, trying to see something more of the insurgents' preparations. Before very long I discovered another detachment, not quite as strong as the first that I had seen on the road, which was moving to the right in the valley below me. This force was accompanied by a long string of pack-animals and a bugler, who from time to time gave vent to weird and brassy calls of his own. Altogether I must have seen close on three thousand men during the day. While we were awaiting the return of our emissary, two "Royal" (Essad Pasha's Own) mounted gendarmes came our way; they joined our group and conversed in the most friendly manner imaginable with the enemy, with whom they appeared to be on visiting terms. I was much surprised at this and wondered what it all meant. Though the gendarmes knew who I was, they did not salute me or show respect, but glowered at me till they left us. It must be said to their credit that they looked a thousand times more villainous than the insurgents.

As time was getting on and the messenger did not return, I decided to make a move and told my friends to send the letter to Durazzo on the next day. I promised them that I would hand it to the King as soon as I received it. Shaking everybody heartily by the hand, to ensure their not shooting me as soon as my back was turned, I got on my pony and left them, accompanied by one of their number. Now they all stood up and saluted respectfully and so did all the other pickets that I passed on my way back to the road; arrived here, my escort, who seems to have been a sort of sergeant among his people, took leave of me and wished me a pleasant ride home. I did not stop to take the part of news-monger, when the worthies of Shjak surrounded me on my return to their village, and rode home at a jog trot.

It had been an interesting experience and, though I had not succeeded in finding out the names of the leaders of insurrection, I felt satisfied in my own mind that Essad was not one of them; besides this it appeared that the rising was not directed against the King's person, but against his ministry. I decided that there were two principal causes for it - religious fanaticism and agrarian discontent.

When I got back to the Palace, I found everybody in a great

state of excitement and the Mbret was so busy that he could not see me for some time. When I made my report to him, he did not appear to take the slightest interest in what I was telling him, or thank me for my trouble. This was rather disheartening, as I was under the impression that I had got some quite useful information for him and done a good day's work.

Chapter Eleven

. . . .

THE COUP D'ÉTAT - 19TH MAY

The reason for everybody's worried expression and the general state of nervous tension, I soon discovered to be the following: when I had left the King in the morning and the Royal cavalcade had kept close to the seashore on the sands, it had met with a rather painful experience. As they were galloping along quite peacefully, the officer in charge of the escort suddenly noticed the glint of rifle-barrels on the top of the Sasso Bianco (or White Cliff, a rocky hill which rises up close to the sea, about half-way to Kavaya, some six kilometres from Durazzo), some thousand yards, or so, in front. A halt was made and then a few figures could be distinguished moving about on the hill; there were only a few of them, but still! It seems probable that these men belonged to the extreme left of the line of pickets I visited during the day. After some deliberation, it was deemed advisable to retire, so the royal party turned tail and rode home at a good canter.

It is possible that, had they ridden on, without taking any notice of the insurgents, or had the King ridden up to them and spoken to them, the whole rebellion might have fizzled out and so all the useless bloodshed might have been avoided! In retiring as he did the King showed weakness; it is true that he was only following the advice of the aide-de-camp, who was supposed to know the ways of his countrymen, but all the same,

he ought to have taken the bull by the horns and attempted to
do something. Doubtless the insurgents presumed that they had
succeeded in frightening him and the tale of their victory
probably went the length and breadth of the country before
that evening. Essad Pasha was immediately sent for and cross-
examined; he still painted everything in rosy colours and
laughed at the incident. He did not believe that there was any
danger of a serious rising and made several palpably false
statements. Anyway the King's interview with him was so
unsatisfactory, that by the time that I got home in the
afternoon, nearly everybody was firmly convinced that Essad
was a traitor, and that Durazzo would be taken by his supporters
during the night.

No one listened to what I had to tell, as it was considered
quite certain that Essad was the root of all evil; only Castoldi
was interested in it, though he too was very disturbed that day.
Perhaps he knew what we only suspected: that Essad Pasha was
hand in glove with the Italian government, and he may have
been afraid that unpleasant disclosures might be made, if steps
were taken to break the Italians' protégé.

In the course of the evening things became rather mixed
and nobody knew what to expect next. Durazzo was divided
into two rival camps; nearly everybody was against the minister
for War and thought that he was going to undertake a coup de
main during the night, get possession of the town and force the
King to leave the country. The Italians and a small band of his
retainers supported him loyally, but were in the minority. At a
late hour we heard that Essad Pasha had ordered the Dutch
Commandant of the town, Major Johan Sluys, to hand over the
guns to an unknown new man, whom he had nominated as
Commandant of the artillery. When this news spread abroad, it
created a panic as people took this to be a sure sign that Essad
was going to play some hanky-panky during the night. As
Essad's nominee was an Italian by origin, the Austrians
naturally enough did not attempt to pacify the people, so the
feeling in the town became more and more nervous as time
went on. It was rumoured that Captain Moltedo, the officer in

question, was in Essad's pay and as the King had absolute confidence in the Dutchman, he did not confirm Moltedo's appointment.[25] Essad Pasha and Major Sluys almost came to blows over this incident.

To show how excited people were that night it is sufficient to tell the following story, which was circulated after the above-mentioned interview and believed by everybody, though nobody knew who had started it and it seems incredible - even for Albania! It is said that when Sluys visited Essad's house to protest against Moltedo's appointment, Essad ordered one of his retainers to put some poison into the major's coffee; the man is supposed to have refused to do so, saying that he would not mind shooting him, but that to poison a man was beneath his dignity. Essad waited till the Major had left and then shot his servant dead; as there were naturally no witnesses to this domestic disturbance and no corpse was found on the premises some hours later, the whole story was doubtlessly a fabrication.

As far as I remember the outcome of the King's decision to support Major Sluys was the resignation of the Minister for War, who felt himself slighted. Everybody was glad to hear that the artillery would remain in reliable hands and flocked round the popular Dutch officer. Our garrison at this time consisted of about a hundred gendarmes, who however could not be entirely relied upon, as they were mostly natives of the affected districts and had joined the force before the King's arrival, when Essad was still in the saddle. As a "precautionary measure", Major Sluys armed about 150 Nationalists and other loyalists in the town, thus raising our armed forces to roughly 250 men.

In the course of the evening a plot was formed to draw Essad's fangs; as a matter of fact the plot was so neatly hidden, that the proceedings later on in the night took quite a legal aspect.

In Albania it is customary for a gentleman to keep a certain number of armed followers always handy, partly to protect him from the emissaries of his enemies and partly to impress the population with his power and importance. As Durazzo was now supposed to be a part of Europe, most of the notables had limited their number of their retinue to two or three men. Essad however did not take part in this general demobilisation, but kept a villainous-looking company of cut-throats; some at his house and the main body in an old Venetian tower on the hill. There were supposed to be about a hundred and twenty of them altogether; quite an imposing force and certainly the most warlike people in the town. As Essad was suspected of harbouring treasonable designs, these men naturally constituted a grave danger to the peace of the town. It was therefore decided to disarm them and render them harmless; Essad was to be charged with keeping a private army, which, people said, was in itself illegal and should he offer resistance, he was to be taken, dead or alive. The undertaking was planned and organised by Nationalists and foreigners, most of whom were in the service of the Albanian government. As things turned out, I am glad to say that I had nothing to do with it, though had I known anything about it, I would probably have joined in, as I honestly believed that the King could do nothing as long as Essad remained in the country. I spent the evening in the house, looking after the Queen and the ladies-in-waiting, who were staying up, as there was no doubt that something exciting was going to happen during the night. The general belief was, as I have already mentioned, that the town would be attacked; this view I could not share, as I felt certain that the rebels were not Essad's men, in spite of their friendliness with the mounted gendarmes.

At about 11 o'clock I saw Faik Bey Konitza from my window and called out to him to ask him what was happening in the town; his answer: "Nothing yet!" was the first indication we got that something was going to be undertaken by our people. The King had a very busy time, as ministers and other officials kept coming in to bother him; the Italian destroyer flotilla arrived and the senior officer came to enquire what he could do for us. A signal of distress was arranged with him, on seeing which the ships in the harbour were to land detachments, to protect the Palace. Worn out with worry, the King seems to have gone to sleep in his study - anyway he did not hear a gun being brought through the garden, right under his window, at about midnight. The Queen, ladies, Ekrem and I, still blissfully ignorant of what was going on all round, amused ourselves as best we could and awaited developments. When Sami Bey had ushered out the King's last visitor, he had himself retired to his house in the town, as usual; as he was Essad's son-in-law some of us thought his conduct very suspicious and imagined that he had gone to Essad's house to plot with him. As it turned out afterwards Sami, who did not believe in his father-in-law's guilt or the probability of a night attack, acted in perfectly good faith and spent the rest of the night in innocent and refreshing sleep; even the firing of the gun did not disturb his slumbers.

At last, at about three o'clock in the morning, a bey came to tell us about the plot and warned the Queen that there would probably be some firing later on, as he thought that Essad would resist arrest; it was a chilly night and he was glad to get a cup of coffee before setting out again to rejoin Major Sluys. As dawn was breaking, we heard a couple of rifle shots in the distance, which were followed by a fusillade; then there was a loud report, which woke up all the innocents in the town and rattled the window panes. So the gun was at work! A second and third shot followed in quick succession and then everything was still again. After the first shots I ran to the King, who was much disturbed by the shooting and did not know what was happening. I told him what I knew and he sent me to signal to the ships from the top balcony; this was a wise precaution, as we did not know whether the arrest would be successful and, had Essad been victorious, there might have been severe trouble in the town. Within a quarter of an hour sailors were landed and took up defensive positions in the garden and by the main approaches from the town. However peace had already been restored and the first warriors were returning from the "battle", to bring us the news of Essad's surrender. In due course, Major Sluys who had been in charge of the "arrest", arrived at the Palace to make a verbal report to the King on the night's happenings; the following is roughly what he said:

"It was brought to my notice that Essad Pasha kept a large body-guard of armed men in Durazzo. As amongst his retainers there were men of notorious character, such as Osman Bali[7], and as Essad himself is suspected of attempting to overthrow the Government; I, as Commandant of the town, felt it my duty to break up the gang and demand its immediate surrender. I ordered Essad's house to be surrounded and had a gun trained on it from a suitable position behind the Palace; I called upon Essad's men to lay down their arms and as they were about to comply with my order, their master appeared on the scene and asked me who had authorised me to give the order. When I told him that I had given the order on my own responsibility, he called upon his men to take up their arms again and prepare for resistance. A shot was fired and in the ensuing volleys one of our men was wounded. As I did not wish to endanger the lives of our men, I ordered the gun to open fire. The first shot blew a hole in the roof of the house and after the third, which burst in Essad Pasha's bedroom, he had nothing left but to surrender."

Major Sluys now wanted to know what he was to do: was Essad to be lodged in the gaol, on board the Austrian cruiser which had been offered for this purpose, or what else was to be done with him?

Chapter Twelve

ESSAD ARRESTED AND RELEASED

As the King had only heard of the plot against Essad after it had already been carried out, he did not now know what to do with him; he could not even make up his mind whether he was to arrest him formally or not. He felt that the War Minister had been wronged but was not strong enough to strike out on a course of his own. Had no outside influence been brought to bear on him, it is probable that he would have had Essad brought to the palace as a free man; however outside influence was brought to bear on him and after a lengthy discussion, it was decided to send Essad on board the Austro-Hungarian cruiser, "Szigetvar". The Austrian authorities had promised to deliver him up, if called upon to do so by the King. Major Sluys had hardly left the house when the King, urged by the Queen, changed his mind, deciding to send Essad to the prison instead. I was sent to notify the Major of the King's decision. On my return to the palace I found that new influences had been at work during my absence and that the original order was to be carried out after all; so I had to get hold of Sluys whose remarks about this continual change of plan were rather sarcastic. I did not like the idea of sending a political prisoner onto a foreign warship, as I was afraid of renewed Austro-Italian differences on the subject; besides it struck me as rather irregular that a political prisoner should be, practically, extradited and then handed back to the authorities of his own country by a foreign power. Of course it did not make any great difference to anybody whether I approved or disapproved of the scheme!

At 9 o'clock an Austro-Italian naval detachment was ready to escort me up to Essad Pasha's house, where I was to arrest him and bring him back safely to the landing-stage. The dragomen from the Austrian and Italian legations accompanied me to act as interpreters and to see fair play. It was a most unpleasant business and, as I was tired after my ride to the insurgents on the previous day and a night out of bed, I did not appreciate it at all, particularly as I thought it probable that Essad's bodyguard, which had surrendered, but not yet been disarmed, would open fire on us as soon as we got through the great gateway, close to the house. As I was walking in front, I felt anything but brave.

On arriving at the house, the two dragomen and I went up to the door, more than expecting a volley to send us into the next world; the Italian dragoman, I suppose, knew that we were safe enough and was therefore not surprised when the door was immediately opened to us. In the hall stood Essad and his wife, with their retainers all round them - and the Court Doctor Berghausen. What the latter was doing here we could not find out; probably he had only come on some pretext, in order to watch the arrest and join the procession, as he liked to appear before the public as a person of great importance, he was much annoyed that I would not allow him to accompany us down to the landing-stage. Essad, who seemed to know what to expect, was not at all surprised when I informed him that he was under arrest and would have to accompany me down to the landing-stage, where he would be handed over to the commander of the Austrian cruiser. His wife, who was devoted to him, begged to be permitted to go with him, and as this did not clash with my orders, and appeared to be a reasonable request, I without hesitation permitted her to do so. Essad's enemies afterwards told me that he only took his wife with him as a protection; the Albanians are very chivalrous and would hesitate to murder a man in the presence of his wife. As I had reason to believe that

Essad's life was in danger, the Italian commander of the escort and I took the couple between us. I did not want to take Essad through the palace garden, and had intended going down to the harbour through the town, the shorter way. However Essad was very anxious not to go through the town and as I had no definite instructions we took the garden route. Later on in the day I discovered that three men had been posted at windows, overlooking the road we were expected to take, and that Essad would have been murdered had he walked into the trap. The conspirators were very disappointed at the turn of events and bore me some ill-will, saying that I had compromised the King by bringing Essad through his garden. Probably Essad had received a warning that he would not reach the harbour alive if he went through the town; there cannot have been any other reasons for his preferring the indirect route. We met very few people on the way, as we were expected to pass through the town, and the square in front of the palace had been cleared by the police; as we reached this and crossed it to the landing stage, the crowds assembled behind the gateway leading to the town set up a howl, so I kept well in front of Essad, to prevent anybody from taking a shot at him. I was criticised for bringing him the way I did, but I am glad that I did so, as it is certain that he would have been murdered, had we gone through the town. At the landing-stage I handed him over to Captain Schmidt of the "Szigetvar"; here Essad assured me that he had been loyal to the throne throughout and that he was the victim of an intrigue. From the time of his arrest till we parted company he had behaved with great dignity and sang-froid under most trying circumstances, so in spite of the fact that I believed him to be a traitor, I had to admire his conduct and feel sympathy for him in his fall. A launch was waiting for him; he got in and so disappeared, officially at least, from the public life of the Six Month Kingdom!

As he was leaving I noticed two of his retainers, who had accompanied him with his hand-luggage, trying to get away unnoticed in the crowd; I caught them up before they had gone very far, arrested them and handed them over to the Palace

Guard, who transferred them to the congenial atmosphere of the gaol. They were a couple of very nasty-looking blackguards and as everybody connected with Essad was now suspected of being a criminal, their disappearance may have saved them from the vengeance of the mob!

During the day everything was upside down: ministers quarrelled in the street, surrounded by riff-raff; the cabinet resigned and the palace was strongly guarded by foreign sailors; they stood about the passages and stairs for hours on end, guarding the entrances and doors of half the rooms in the house. Why they had been called in, or against whom, nobody exactly knew and the Italians laughed at such elaborate precautions! After a time it was considered sufficient for them to take up the duties of the palace guards, who, though they had behaved irreproachably all the time, were considered too unreliable; so our corridors were evacuated and the house once again belonged to us.

Essad's house was searched and several trunks full of documents were taken from there to the police-station, where they remained, I believe for ever afterwards without being opened. Several other houses, belonging to Essad's friends, were also searched and numerous arrests were made by the over-zealous police; however no shred of evidence could be found against anybody and most of the victims were released later on in the day. In the afternoon great discussions took place as to what we were to do with Essad, now that we had got him; some proposed that he should get a fair trial, enthusiasts wanted him to be brought back and hanged in the square, and the Italians considered that he should be permitted to retire from public life and to live in Italy. I personally proposed a court martial composed of foreign officers serving under the Albanian government; for instance von Trotha as president, Major Sluys and I as members.

To our great disgust, we were told next day that the Italians had prevailed and that Essad would be sent into exile, without a trial. I was annoyed at this decision as I failed to see how the Mbret had the right to send a man into exile, whose guilt had not been proved. I told the King that he was hastening his own downfall by allowing Essad to go abroad, from where he was certain to take vengeance for the manner in which he had been treated. I felt certain that Essad was guilty and wanted it proved; in that case a court would have been justified in sentencing him to death and so the whole matter would have ended. As it was, the King's decision, which neither acquitted nor condemned his late most powerful minister, made an exceedingly bad impression on his loyal subjects; they considered that the King had robbed them of their prey and had allowed himself to be outwitted by the Italian diplomats, who were generally believed to be Essad Pasha's allies.

At midday I was sent on board the "Szigetvar" to communicate the Mbret's decision to the victim and also to search his luggage and confiscate all documents in his possession, a useless precaution, as a man of Essad's intelligence would not have been fool enough to carry incriminating papers about with him! According to my instructions to seize all papers, I brought away three attaché-cases full, which were sealed by him and delivered to the Mbret on my return to the palace. One of my last official duties before leaving Durazzo in August, was to return these cases, the seals unbroken, to Essad Pasha's address in Italy; as they were never looked into, what on earth was the use of having sent me to take them from him?

Essad also had to sign a promise that he would not attempt to return to the country without the Mbret's permission to do so, and that he would not in any manner, privately or publicly, mix himself up in Albanian politics or intrigues against the throne; this promise he signed without any hesitation. He again assured me of his loyalty and said that the King would regret his hasty action and recall him, when he would willingly return to work for the good of his country. We parted friends and Essad Pasha left for the Italian port of Bari in an Italian ship late in the afternoon. I wonder whether he took it all so well because he knew that the King would not be able to hold out much longer and that he himself would soon be in the saddle again?

That evening there was a new excitement in the town; in fact half the population thought that the end had come! The two hundred men of Kruja had arrived from Shjak; why nobody exactly knew as they had received no orders to come to Durazzo; it was generally believed that they were Essad's most devoted followers and that they had come to wreak vengeance on the town. Ekrem Bey Libohova took a very serious view of this new complication and was of the opinion that the town was really in danger as long as these warriors were at large, so, in spite of their protestations of loyalty, they were locked up overnight in the school house, strongly guarded by Nationalist volunteers. Next morning they were released and, in spite of the rather curious treatment that they had received, made a loyal demonstration outside the palace, after which they were allowed to leave the town unmolested and return to their native district.

Although the Kruja men were safely under lock and key, it was thought advisable to arm our servants; I took the matter in hand, and putting von Trotha's secretary, a non-commissioned officer in the German Foot Guards, in charge, I served out rifles and ammunition to all the men-servants. Practically all of them had served their time in the Austrian or German army, so they ought to have known how to handle a rifle! However they turned out to be a very second-rate lot of soldiers, as before I had finished arming them one of their number loosed off a round, the bullet burying itself in the wall, not far off the cook's head. I cursed everybody heartily, told them not to load the rifles or play about with them and went upstairs; hardly had I joined the ladies when there was a second loud report, which fairly made us jump. I ran downstairs again and found a group of frightened retainers standing round the cook's assistant, who, rifle in hand, was also shaking with fear and astonishment; he had let off his round into the ceiling, just underneath the corner where the ladies had been sitting. Von Trotha now appeared on the scene in a most unpleasant humour and gave the servants a lecture, in the course of which they heard as choice language as they had ever done while they were in the army. He then disarmed them all, with the exception of the native "Kavasses", as their "protection" appeared to mean the untimely death of one of us before the arrival of an enemy.

This comedy was the last event of any interest during the evening; we sat up late, expecting further alarms, as rumours of threatening disturbances kept coming in, but nothing happened and at a late hour we retired to rest and slept undisturbed till next morning. Unfortunately the Essad incident was now closed; the King made the grave mistake of not having an immediate enquiry made into the whole matter. Had an efficient commission been brought into existence, it is probable that Major Sluys could have justified his action, besides which the charges of treason against Essad might have been gone into and perhaps proved to everybody's satisfaction. As it was, the whole affair remained wrapped in mystery and nobody to this day knows exactly how it originally came about. On thinking the matter over quietly, I believe that foreign influences deserve most of the blame, though at the time I was under the impression that the plot was entirely of Nationalist origin.

The Mbret's actions naturally enough led Essad's supporters to believe that he had known all about the conspiracy against his minister and had approved of the bombardment of his house, and it is not to be wondered at that this made an exceedingly bad impression in the country. The foreign press had the same impression and eulogies were written about the Mbret's "determination", in ridding himself of his unruly minister. It was a bad affair, bungled from beginning to end and did the King's cause a lot of harm. Had a proper enquiry been made into the matter, it seems certain that everybody could have been whitewashed, somehow, and in this case the Mbret would not have lost so much prestige among his subjects.

Chapter Thirteen

. . . .

23RD MAY - FLIGHT

On the 21st May we got very bad news from the interior, particularly from Kavaya and the surrounding districts; we heard that the gendarmerie detachment had been driven out of the town by the populace and that the local barber, or some other individual of the same standing had set himself up as the president of a new republic. The national flag was pulled down and the Turkish one put in its place.

Next day still more disquieting news reached us from Tirana and the governor there wired for reinforcements, as the position was critical. Our garrison was very small, but after a long debate with General De Veer[26] the King decided to send an expedition to Tirana. The Italian and Essad parties for some reason or other thought that this expedition was sent at my instigation; as a matter of fact I had nothing to do with it and the first I knew about it was late in the evening, when the King sent me to the general, to find out whether it had left! The Dutch Captain Jan Sar was sent with a force of 50 gendarmes and 100 Roman Catholic Malissori tribesmen from northern Albania; attached to his force were two foreign sportsmen, Prince Sturdza and the Comte de Pimodan, who were in charge of one mountain-gun and one machine-gun.

When this detachment reached Shjak, the Malissori suddenly informed Sar that they intended going no further, as they had been sent from the North to act as bodyguard to the King and had no wish to leave their bones in central Albania, where they might not even get a Christian burial. Besides, they said that they were wearing their best clothes which they did not intend to spoil for anybody! They were "fed up" and even the entreaties of their leader, Simon Doda, who stuck to the Dutchman like a man, would not move them. As the Malissoris' conduct seemed inexplicable, a reason for it had to be discovered - or invented. So we in due course heard that they had been got hold of by Italian agents, who had told them that they were being led into a trap; that the rebels would wipe them out before they ever reached their destination. We never found out whether there was any truth in the story, but to me it seems not only possible but probable. Sar telegraphed to Durazzo for further instructions, as he considered it madness to attempt to push through with the remaining third of his men. To his astonishment the General De Veer did not share his views and insisted on his advancing, in spite of the smallness of his force. General De Veer probably thought that the force would find no resistance; so far there had been no actual bloodshed and there was really no reason to believe that the rebels would go to extremes. The expedition was meant to be a demonstration and had no orders to attack the insurgents without provocation. As Sar foresaw a catastrophe, he left the mountain-gun at Shjak, thinking that the Malissori could be relied upon to look after it for the present, particularly as there were still a few gendarmes left in the village. He left in the early hours of the morning, but did not get very far before the insurgents attacked from all sides; his gendarmes put up a good fight, but were quite unable to hold their own against the superior numbers of the enemy. Sar hoped that the Malissori on hearing the firing would come to his assistance, but as there was no sign of them and his little band had suffered considerably, he was forced to surrender, the rebels having crept round and cut off his only line of retreat.[27]

This "unfortunate incident" certainly encouraged the insurgents to try their skill at bigger game and so brought on the attack on Durazzo, which caused the catastrophe of the 23rd May. On this day the Mbret lost most of his prestige, but as the reader will see for himself when he reads what happened, there was more in it all than met the eye and the unfortunate Mbret could not very well help acting as he did! "Tout comprendre, c'est tout pardonner."

On waking up on the morning of the 23rd of May, I heard that Sar's Malissori had returned to Durazzo by themselves and that the rest of the troops had been defeated at Shjak and forced to surrender. The Malissori had left the gun at Shjak, as, owing to the approach of large numbers of the insurgents, they had retired in rather a hurry. On getting this news, I jumped into my clothes and went up to the King (who was in his bath) to inform him and receive his instructions; then I went out to try to get further particulars for him. In the palace garden I met the Italian Minister, who seemed very agitated and told me that there were 8,000 fanatics on the way to attack the town. He appeared to think that I was the cause of this and told me that public opinion in Durazzo held me responsible for the sending of the ill-fated expedition; he also insinuated that something would happen to me if I did not leave Durazzo immediately and warned me as a friend to get out of it as quickly as possible. As an ordinary non-Albanian is not in the habit of having "things happening to him", I was frightened, knowing that orientals become very rough at times, when things are not going smoothly. Besides, several people had already warned me that Essad Pasha's friends bore me some ill-will for the part I had played in his arrest, and ill-will is in Albania the first cousin of blood feud; so really I had some reason to feel nervous! I walked across the square with shaky knees and on reaching the old Venetian tower behind the custom-house wiped the cold sweat off my forehead, glad to be away from the crowd, which I imagined would soon follow me and tear me to pieces. A clear conscience may be an excellent thing in its way, but on this occasion it did not give me any comfort. From the corner, by the old tower, one could get an excellent view of the Tirana road and the heights of Raspul, which an enemy coming from the interior would have to cross before attacking the town; so I sat there looking across the water and the swamps through my field-glasses. After a while I could hear firing in the distance, an echo from the far side of the hills; then a few men came trooping down the Tirana road. At first I hoped that they might be some of Sar's men, but soon my hopes were shattered; the firing came closer and closer, and further stronger detachments, which could only be the insurgents' advance-guard, appeared on the sky-line on both sides of the road. Our outposts were soon driven in and fell back on the main line of resistance, near the bridge, where about seventy of our men, commanded by a young German ex-officer, Baron Gumppenberg, were holding our right flank. Gumppenberg was originally a subaltern in the German cavalry, which he left owing to some disagreement with the authorities. He then joined the Turkish army, with which he served during the Tripoli war and a part of the Balkan war. At von Trotha's instigation, he was given a commission in the Albanian militia and the gallant fight that he put up during this first day of war with his irregulars did more than anything else to save Durazzo. He was slightly wounded during the day, but this did not prevent him from trying to charge the rebels, estimated at 1,500 men, in the afternoon, when his men had to cease fire for a time owing to lack of ammunition.

I reported my observations to the King and then returned to my post, as there was nothing to keep me in the house for the time being. At about 11 o'clock the artillery opened fire; one of the Austrian guns had been unpacked and used against Essad's house on the morning of the 19th and this was now at our disposal. As the Austrian officers, who had come to instruct the Albanians how to use it, were not allowed to leave their ship, I believe for political reasons,[28] we had to do the best we could with volunteers. The first Albanian artillery was, as far as I can remember, manned by Ekrem Bey Vlora, a couple of German commercial travellers and an Austrian waiter; none of these knew very much about gunnery and the result was that several shells were badly fused and exploded over the town. However they soon improved and at the end of the first hour were dropping shells onto the insurgents' lines quite successfully.

Altogether we had about 250 men under arms; about 150 of these were in the firing-line under Major Roelfsema and Baron Gumppenberg and the remainder were kept in reserve. Several European civilians, who happened to be in Durazzo on business, did more than their share in the work; particularly the Austrians and Germans, who behaved very creditably all through; a young Englishman, Mr. Walford,[29] acted as galloper to the General. Only the Italians were conspicuous by their absence; though the town was full of them, they did not attempt to take any part in its defence.

As I was returning to the palace at midday, I again met the Italian Minister, who repeated his warning to me and this time represented my danger as being so great that he advised me to get away to the Italian warship in a boat, without even returning to the palace to get my things. This second warning was even more serious than the first and I found it necessary to visit the butler for a glass of brandy to keep me going. I was kept busy after lunch and nothing of interest happened till about 3 o'clock, when Baron Aliotti arrived at the palace; he now informed the King that in his opinion the position had deteriorated, that he would have to withdraw his naval detachment, which, with the Austrian, was guarding the palace, as he could not endanger the lives of the Italian sailors. As I received him, Aliotti said he had come to save the King, but that, as I had ignored his warnings, it was too late for me. His advice was that the King, Queen and children should retire to the "Misurata", as a massacre would probably follow the insurgents' entry into Durazzo. The Austrian Minister was sent for and, though he had seemed quite optimistic about everything in the morning, he now shared his colleague's views and also advised the King to escape, as quickly as possible. Something must have taken place between the two ministers, something that we knew nothing about, as I feel convinced that Herr von Löwenthal did not himself see any reason for our leaving the Palace and was against our doing so, even though he officially had to support the Italian proposal.

It has already been mentioned that the Mbret was not a strong man, so one cannot be surprised to hear that he allowed himself to be persuaded by the diplomatic representatives of "Albania's godparents". What else was he to do? The chances are that "something" would have happened to him, if he had attempted to see the whole thing through, regardless of the advice of the two most influential ministers! The worst devils of International Politics were abroad that day - with a vengeance - and no one could foresee what would happen next!

As a final coup de grace Aliotti snarled at me that, not having taken note of his former warnings, it was now too late for me to get away. Of course the continual warnings so unnerved me that I was quite unable to give the King any sensible advice, or do anything useful. This, I verily believe, was their object. Had the Aide-de-camp or I only ridden out to the bridge to look at things ourselves the flight might never have taken place at all! For my part I must admit that I was thoroughly shaken.

The King had to give way and that was the end of it; when the ministers had made their departure and I was left alone with him, the poor man was quite white and at his wits' end. As he ordered me to arrange for a hasty departure, to get the trunks packed and servants ready, there were tears in his eyes and I was really sorry for him, particularly as he had always been kindness itself to me and had done everything to make me comfortable. He looked round the study and sighed "It seems such a pity to have to leave all my old things here; why must it be?" As I was not in a particularly cheerful state of mind myself and did not want to let him see my emotion, I answered rather abruptly "Well, it was bound to come sooner or later, so we had better make the best of a bad job!" and left him, perhaps rather taken aback by such impertinence.

After giving the necessary instructions to the servants, I helped the King to pack some of his valuables and the Essad Pasha papers, then going to my own room to pack my dressing-case. I put in everything that I really valued, jewellery, keep-sakes and about £50 of money and deposited it in the passage outside my room. At that moment von Trotha came along with two bags containing 40,000 francs in gold, part of the Court funds, for which I had to find room in my dressing-case; this, not having been light at any time, was now so heavy that I could hardly lift, much less carry, it myself. I dragged it to the foot of the stairs, where the other luggage was collected, and left it there, telling one of the servants to keep his eye on it.

Word was sent to us, as far as I remember from the Italian Legation, that we had better hurry up, as the rebels were advancing rapidly and the landing-stage would soon be under fire; a melancholy procession was formed and slowly we marched across the square that had given us such a splendid welcome some ten weeks before. Now all was silent and foreign sailors lined the route! At the landing-stage launches from the "Misurata" were awaiting us and soon afterwards we arrived on board;[30] the servants followed us in due course, with such luggage as there had been time to pack, but my dressing case was nowhere to be found! So the King fled to the ship and the European press had its large headlines for the morning editions!

Before closing this chapter, it is only fair to mention the fact that Sami Bey, the chamberlain, was the only one in the palace who did not loose his head; he considered that the King's flight was unnecessary and advocated his view so forcibly, that there was no longer any doubt about his loyalty. He predicted that the flight would make a bad impression all over the country and begged us to do all in our power to prevent it. Unfortunately he would not speak to the King himself, being too shy to do so; but he wept bitter tears of grief, poor fellow!

Chapter Fourteen

· · · ·

23RD MAY - RETURN

It was quite pleasant to be on board a foreign warship, as one at least felt safe from assassins' bullets; however our joy was short-lived and before very long we were all sorry that we had ever left the land. It was most depressing to see the Royal Standard being lowered on the palace! As a matter of fact this made a very bad impression on the defenders of Durazzo, who had fought all day without any encouragement and were now being left in the lurch by the very man they had been fighting for. We sat about the deck, moping and were thoroughly downhearted at this unpleasant ending to our adventure. Several of us had hoped to remain here in Durazzo for the rest of our lives, and now all our hopes were suddenly dashed to the ground at one fell swoop! I looked after the servants and luggage, hoping to find my dressing-case; however to my great dismay nobody could tell me anything about it. I also discovered that several of the servants, including the English butler, had been left behind at the palace, so I asked the officer in command of the ship to allow me to go back to fetch them in one of his launches. This request he courteously, but firmly refused, as his orders were to let nobody leave the ship for the time being; he could not make an exception for me, as he would be held responsible if anything went wrong. I was also told that my going ashore was out of the question in any case, as the insurgents were already in the town and the risk would be too great.

Sentries with fixed bayonets were posted about the deck, "to prevent undesirable refugees from trying to get on board". In fact we were kept here whether we liked it or not! I was absolutely furious at this and asked the captain whether we were to consider ourselves his prisoners; his answer implied that I could consider myself anything I chose, but that his instructions were not to allow anybody to return to the town. As arguing with the captain of a ship is not a profitable pastime and never does any good, I retired to the boat-deck, where the others were assembled, and from here watched what was happening on land. We got a good view of the swamps and saw our detachments apparently still holding their own round the bridge; the firing had died down and, as far as I could make out through my field-glasses, everything seemed to be in more or less perfect order.

After a time it appears that a truce was called and parliamentaries, headed by old Mehmet Pasha Dralla,[31] went out from the town to talk to the rebels. A motor car, flying a huge Italian flag, scudded to and fro and, I believe, the International Commission of Control also sallied forth to treat for peace. We watched people coming and going and it was damnable to have to sit still and take no part in the proceedings. The King was always a reserved man and on this occasion, as usual, had not told us what he thought of doing next, so we wondered whether we would be taken to some Italian or Austrian port, or whether the King intended going up to Scutari, to try his luck in the North. Most of us hoped for the latter, though the King perhaps was not so keen on restarting his adventure, after the first reverse. I do not think that he had any particular affection for his new subjects; at any rate he had no reason to have any, as so few of them had given him a square deal.

When we had been on the "Misurata" two hours, and had finished our tea, Admiral Trifari, the senior Italian officer in the harbour, came on board with "very important news" for the

King. He remained closed with him in one of the saloons for some time and when they came out together, the King was pale and appeared to be rather agitated. The "important news" was this: the insurgents had defeated us and had practically got possession of the town; however they did not intend to sack it if the King would receive their spokesmen in the palace and treat with them, in person. When the King asked why these spokesmen could not be brought on board the "Misurata", he was informed that they had absolutely refused to come out on the sea. The Mbret did not appear to be at all anxious to leave the ship, as, having come on board in order to avoid massacre, he did not appreciate the idea of putting his head into the noose a second time. However the Admiral urged him to do so and before long we, the King, Ekrem Bey and I were scudding homeward in the Italian motor-boat. The sun had gone down and altogether this was a most unpleasant trip, as we were firmly convinced that we were being led into some sort of trap, out of which we would probably not escape alive. On the square we could distinguish armed figures, but were unable to make out whether they were friends or foes; our hearts throbbed and we expected to be fired upon the moment that we set foot on terra firma. At the landing-stage a pleasant surprise awaited us; instead of being surrounded by villainous insurgents, we found ourselves welcomed by loyalists, who wept with joy at the Mbret's safe return to the capital. On our way across the square, one of them warned me to be careful, as "the Italians were playing some low game", which remark was not so very reassuring. Capitano Castoldi met us in the garden and at our approach the Kavass, who was sitting at the gate with his rifle across his knees, welcomed us with joy and led the way into the house.

The electric light had been switched off at the main and we had to find our way up the stairs as best we could in the dark; as we could no longer make head or tail of anything and had lost confidence in everybody, almost in ourselves, we kept our Brownings ready for immediate action, expecting some evil-disposed persons to leap at us out of the darkness. However in this, too, we were disappointed, as all remained peaceful. In due course candles were brought to us in the passage, outside the King's study, stuck in empty beer bottles (Not very regal, I admit, but the only candlesticks that could be raised for the time being!).

Soon people came pouring in: Ministers, Control Commissioners, officers and loyal beys, but nothing was to be seen of the rebels' emissaries, though we were assured that they might turn up at any moment. We had been here doing nothing in particular for a couple of hours, when I heard someone coming up the stairs; to everybody's great astonishment it turned out to be Captain Sar, who had been captured by the rebels that morning at Shjak! His captors had released him on parole to come in to Durazzo and treat with the Mbret on their behalf. They demanded a letter of amnesty for their past offences, and in return promised not to attack the town for the present; if Sar failed in his mission, or should break his parole, the insurgents threatened to shoot all their prisoners. The King immediately had a letter of amnesty concocted and handed over to Captain Sar, who after telling us his story, was sent back to Shjak in a royal carriage under a flag of truce. It was further arranged that our motor car should be sent there, also under the white flag, to bring in our wounded; however this could not be done immediately, as our chauffeur was still on board the "Misurata".

As the Italians, who appeared to know everything, at this point assured the King that all danger was now past and the town safe from further attack, I was sent on board to fetch off the Queen, ladies and staff. The Queen was an exceedingly plucky woman, but when she saw me arriving without her husband, it gave her an awful shock. She was soon reassured and more than delighted to be able to return to land and take up the fight again. The royal children had been sent on board the "Szigetvar" during the morning and did not return to the palace till next afternoon.

When we got back, the lights in the house were again working and my room was brightly illuminated; through the window we saw Castoldi by my desk, which rather surprised us, as relations between him and myself had been rather strained since the Essad "coup", in which he firmly believed that I had been implicated. Besides this, we had had further unpleasantness between us owing to some over-truthful remark about some of his countrymen in Durazzo, which I had made in an unguarded moment that morning.

We sat down to a cold supper, which had been prepared in all haste, and a glass of champagne, the best tonic in the world, soon raised our spirits; however our troubles were not yet over and another blow was in store for us that night! The meal was hardly over, when Ekrem Bey was called away; he came back with a very long face and the unpleasant news that the Italian and Austrian Ministers had decided to withdraw their detachments. This was certainly most awkward, as the gendarmerie were not to be trusted and they would be the only men left to guard the palace, if the sailors were withdrawn; now it was doubly awkward, having the ladies with us! So Ekrem was sent off to the two Ministers and, after a lot of negotiations, it was finally arranged that the Italians would give us a double guard of 150 men, as the Austrian Minister absolutely declined to furnish us with the usual detachment. The curious thing is that the Austrians, in spite of their refusal, landed a detachment with a machine gun, which remained by the landing stage all night, ready for immediate action. We were never able to discover what caused all the trouble that night, but I was told by an absolutely reliable person in authority, that, had the Austrians furnished us with the usual guard that night this might have led to a catastrophe. Their detachment by the landing stage was a precautionary measure, as it was thought probable that a second flight would be forced upon us during the night.

As the Austrians were very friendly disposed towards the throne and always did all they could to give the poor Mbret the support, which had been promised to him by the Concert of Europe, I feel certain that they had some very serious reasons for not giving us their usual detachment that night. In fact, my personal opinion is that the relations between Austria and Italy were so strained that the slightest incident might have brought about a disaster. The ships in the harbour were kept ready for immediate action and I know that the naval officers of both countries were burning to get at each other's throats.

As arranged, we sent our car over to Shjak to bring in the wounded; two Austrian naval doctors rigged up a hospital in our "dependence", where the Doctor Berghausen, who had already left the King's service, had lived. Everybody was worn out and glad to get to bed, so it was not long before I found myself alone. At about 1 o'clock the car returned, carrying three or four of our men who had been wounded in the morning; they all had serious injuries and we had some difficulty in carrying them up the narrow stairs, but they were brave and uncomplaining; one of them, a young Mirdite, whose leg had been smashed by a dum-dum, even cracked jokes with us as we lifted him out of the car. It was after 2 o'clock when I at last turned in, absolutely tired out after the most unpleasant day that one can well imagine.

I have tried to give an accurate account of what took place and have not attempted to give any sort of explanation; the reader must form his own opinion on the day's happenings. Why we were made to flee to the "Misurata" we could not make out; still less were we able to understand why we were hustled back to the palace by the very people who had driven us out of it. Certain it is that the King's prestige was gone for ever after, and that from this day onward he was practically a dependent of Italy and Austria!

I must still add a word about my dressing-case, which disappeared for good. As Italian sailors kept off the crowd, while the luggage was being transported from the palace to the ship, it is practically certain that my bag was not stolen by any ordinary individual. It did not remain in the palace; that also I know. As it had my name on it and was very heavy, an outsider might have thought that it contained documents; the Essad papers were by some parties considered the most important in our possession. To me it seems probable that some 'agent' was the culprit! What a disappointment to find no papers; maybe a still greater personal satisfaction to find the store of gold coin.

Chapter Fifteen

. . . .

END OF THE MONTH

In the last two chapters I have attempted to describe the happenings on the 23rd of May, but it seems only fair to say a few words in defence of the Mbret's conduct on that day. His flight to the "Misurata" was adversely commented upon in almost the entire foreign press and the King was depicted as an arrant coward; not knowing the full facts of the case, Europe took it upon herself to laugh at him. Everybody who was on the spot and more or less knew what was going on, can testify that his line of conduct was imposed upon him by a "force majeure" and that he was in no sense a free agent.

The representatives of the Great Powers have tremendous influence at small courts and can bring such pressure to bear on a petty ruler, or his government, so that it is absolutely impossible to hold out against them for any length of time. They can adopt a tone which would be more suited to a cab-shelter than to a council chamber; they can cajole, insult, threaten, at their own sweet will, and in the end their word is law. Might is right in international politics, as in everything else! If the reader will bear this in mind, he will judge the King less harshly; had he been a really great man, it is true, he might have acted differently; but he was not a great man, had little self-assurance and no practical training, and his position was very precarious.

The remainder of the month passed off uneventfully and what happened during the next week or two can be told in a few words. The International Commission of Control, which only appeared on the scene when there was some serious difficulty to be surmounted, went over to Shjak on the 25th May to negotiate with the rebels; the Austrian member, Consul-general Kral[32] distinguished himself on this occasion, haranguing the crowd in their own language, which he spoke fluently but which most of his colleagues could not understand. The result of this first visit was not unfavourable; the insurgents received the Commission courteously and agreed to send us back their prisoners and the guns they had captured from Sar's force. The prisoners were returned next day, but the authorities forgot to send over ponies for the guns; this quite annoyed the insurgents, who did not see why they should keep the guns any longer. As a matter of fact ponies were never sent to Shjak and the result was that the rebels kept our guns, finally using them against Durazzo. None of the leaders appeared on this, or any other similar occasion, and the dummy spokesmen present at the meeting had to refer everything to the "Great Ones" who appeared to rule their flock with a rod of iron. It was never discovered who these "Great Ones" were! The general impression brought away by the Commissioners was that the people had been worked up by Young-Turkish agitators; they appeared to have no definite grievances, but wanted the old Turkish regime back, which proposal no halfway educated Albanian would ever have supported, or even tolerated.

It was very noticeable during these days that the insurgents were on excellent terms with the Italians; motor cars used to take out Italian officials and others to Shjak regularly, and it was also remarked that the disloyal elements in the town kept in close touch with various Italians, not wholly unconnected with the legation. We started a sort of secret police to watch political suspects, but, as most of its members were ardent nationalists, with strong Austrian sympathies, we sometimes found it very difficult to separate truth from fiction in their reports. In spite of these little difficulties, we knew much of what was going on in the town; however no arrests were made for the present.

I was told on excellent authority that the Italian legation had requested the King to dismiss both von Trotha and myself, "as we had intrigued against Italian interests". However the King backed us up loyally on this occasion and refused to accede to the Italian demand. The Italians in Durazzo showed me that I was a "Persona ingrata" to them and rather ostracised me until the outbreak of war in August, when there was not enough they could do for me. I received several further warnings to be on my guard, as the Essad party would never forgive me for arresting their leader and then searching his luggage. Von Trotha and Major Sluys were warned in a similar manner; the former was now sent to Germany on a political mission and the latter was allowed to retire to Holland for a few weeks' leave in order to let things blow over. As I had not yet got over my first fright, I got Mr. Lamb,[33] the British member of the International Commission of Control, to find out from Baron Aliotti what reasons he had had for believing me to be in danger and for advising me to leave the country. The latter was rather taken aback and said that he had heard that the Nationalists were displeased with me and wanted to remove me, though he did not know any details. As the Nationalists were the King's most loyal supporters and without exception very friendly-disposed towards myself, I put the whole story down as a down-right lie; without a doubt it was a diplomatic method of preventing me from making myself useful to the King on the 23rd. If so, it was certainly successful and all credit is due to the wily diplomat who engineered it! Had I not been frightened on that occasion, I would most certainly have ridden out to see what was going on at the front, as I did regularly on every subsequent occasion!

One evening, as I was on the point of retiring to bed, I was informed that one of our wounded had died in the Court hospital. As the ADC who was still up, did not care about the job, although, being a Mahommedan and Albanian he could have done it much better than myself, I had to arrange for the man's burial and to send for an "Imam" to pray by the body through the night. The priest's price for a night out of bed was, if I remember rightly, twenty francs; however it was money well spent, as it did the King good among his Mahommedan subjects to appear as the protector of their faith, particularly at a time when the insurgents stated that the government was trying to do away with the Mahommedan religion altogether!

Next afternoon I had to attend the funeral of a young Austrian reserve officer, who had been killed in the fighting of the 23rd; half his head having been blown away by a dum-dum. As I represented the King, I had to walk immediately behind the roughly made coffin; blood kept trickling through the cracks onto the dusty road - great black drops! To me, as yet quite unaccustomed to the horrors of war, this was a most unpleasant duty.

Towards the end of the month the Commissioners of Control again took up negotiations with the insurgents and drove out to Kavaya, where they were quite well received. Now the rebels would not have anything to do with the Mbret or his government, as the story seems to have been spread amongst them that my master was a blood-thirsty tyrant, who killed his subjects for sport. A more ridiculous accusation is hardly imaginable to anybody who knew the "Tyrant", who was as gentle and kindly a man as ever breathed! However amongst the ignorant peasants it was of course believed, and liberally made use of by the unscrupulous agitators. Here the movement appeared to be more fanatical than at Shjak and the Turkish flag was flying on the more important houses in the town. Negotiations were found to be impossible and the Commission returned to Durazzo rather crestfallen.

After the Essad Pasha troubles the whole cabinet retired en bloc and Turkhan Pasha formed a new one, in which one or two of the original members were again included. Essad Pasha's post as Minister of the Interior was filled by a new man, Akif Pasha Elbasani, whom I believe to have been an honourable man, though perhaps not a very able one; Monsieur Philip Nogga[34] took over the finances of the state, and Abdi Bey

Toptani became Minister for Agriculture; the other changes were of minor importance.

After the eventful night of the 18th May, the "Cabinet Royale" kept itself very much in the background and we hardly ever saw either Castoldi or Buchberger; for some time already they had not go on very well with each other and now they spent most of their time in, or about, their respective legations. This position being entirely ludicrous, the King decided to dissolve this Privy Council, on the ground that it was no longer considered a useful organ of government. Its two members were thanked for "the great services that they had rendered the country" and were decorated with the "Order of the Albanian Eagle". We were all sorry for Buchberger, as he had always been put in the shade by his more pushing colleague and we believed that he had played an absolutely straight game and worked for Albania's good throughout. Until the crisis of the 18th May, we had great confidence in Castoldi's ability, but from that day his manner suddenly changed, our relations became more than strained and nobody missed him when he left. He was certainly a strong man, an astute diplomat and pleasant companion, but we all felt that he had not forgotten that he was an Italian and had worked for his country's good more than for Albania's, and this we looked upon as treason towards the King who had trusted him implicitly. I say that we felt this; we had no proofs and possibly we were mistaken.

On the night of the 29th, just as we were going to bed, two shots rang out through the night; as they were fired at no great distance from the palace, they caused a certain amount of alarm. The two naval detachments (the Austrians had sent theirs, as usual, after the night of the 23rd.) were called to arms. From my window I watched the Italians at work; the men acted quickly and well and put the main road leading into the town into a state of defence within a few minutes, a most creditable display. The only pity is that all these preparations were for nothing; there was no riot or mutiny and it was eventually discovered that the two shots had been fired at a stray dog by one of the Dutch officers out of the window of his quarters at the Hotel Clementi. It appeared to me rather a foolish thing to do in a town which was in a state of siege and under military law! However no more was heard about the incident, so it must be buried with the many other follies that became almost a part of our existence in that out of the way corner of the world!

Chapter Sixteen

. . . .

INTRIGUE AND REBELLION

On the 1st of June seven hundred Mirdites and Malissori tribesmen arrived from Alessio,[35] where Prenk Bib Doda Pasha was supposed to be collecting a large army of tribesmen, which, it was hoped, would overawe the insurgents and bring them to their senses. Most of the men were armed with a rifle of sorts and by far the majority of them had fairly modern weapons - Mannlichers and Mausers. The more old-fashioned Martini was also well represented, as its loud report made it popular among the primitive tribesmen, who still believe in instilling terror into their enemies by noise. All these warriors were wearing their picturesque national kit, which however cannot be described as very practical for war, as the baggy white trousers make splendid targets for the enemy's sharpshooters. Unfortunately the Albanian government could not afford to put its soldiers into uniform; our forces cost us quite enough money without that luxury!

This detachment was accompanied by the Bishop of Alessio, a real fighting priest of the old school, who was untiring in looking after and cheering on his turbulent flock.[36] The nominal leader of this expeditionary force was Marco Gioni, a cousin of Prenk's, who however had very little influence with his men and preferred the cafe to the trenches.

On the same boat as our new garrison was also my

brother,[37] who had come out from England to pay me a flying visit. He had made friends with many of the notables on board, conversing with them in a "lingua franca" invented on the spur of the moment. His monocle made a great impression on the simple-minded mountaineers, who had never seen such a wonderful thing in their lives and greatly respected the owner of what was probably a powerful charm! I got him a room at the Hotel Clementi for a day or two, which he however had to share with a stranger; as he did not care about paying 16 francs a day for such inadequate accommodation, the King allowed me to have a tent pitched for him in the precincts of the palace, in which he was far more comfortable. As soon as he heard that there was fighting in the air, he gave up all thoughts of returning home and settled down to learn all he could about the working of the guns. In the course of a few days he had picked up quite a lot about it and was by general consent admitted to be one of the greatest artillery experts in the town! The King and Queen were exceedingly kind to him, for which I was most grateful to them, and he spent what little spare time he had in the palace.

The International Commission went out to Shjak again, but this time the behaviour of the insurgents was barely courteous and their attitude quite unconciliatory. Their demands were now unacceptable, for they insisted that the Mbret must leave the country and a Mahommedan Prince be put in his place. Under these conditions, further negotiation became impossible and all hope of making a compromise faded away; so it was decided to put down the insurrection by force of arms. Everybody thought that this would be a comparatively simple matter and certainly nobody anticipated absolute disaster!

A plan of campaign was worked out in the King's study, which looked very well on paper and would probably have worked admirably if our troops had been highly trained men, instead of armed marauders. It was as follows: we were to advance on the insurgents from all sides, surround their forces and starve them into submission. It was hoped that bloodshed would be avoided and that the insurgents would be cowed into submission and lay down their arms and return to their homes.

In the north was Prenk Bib Doda with his Mirdites and Malissori tribesmen; exactly how many men he had at his disposal at this time we never found out, but I believe that the government was paying for 5,000 to 7,000 men for some time, though it is generally believed that the force assembled did not ever reach so large a figure. In the north-east Ahmed Bey Mati (later, King Zog[38]) had collected a force of some 2,000 of his feudal retainers, with which he was to advance on Tirana, now the centre of the disturbed area, after occupying Kruja. In the east there was a smaller force of Loyalists, having its base at Elbasan and there were two southern armies, one at Berat and the other at Valona. All these forces were to work together and according to plans would drive the rebels back and surround them somewhere between Tirana and Shjak. What happened to all these armies will be told later on, but the less said about it the better, as unfortunately not a single one of them did anything creditable.

It was decided at this council of war to send a couple of guns to Valona; also one to Alessio to encourage Prenk Bib Doda as it was thought that valour was not the strongest trait in his character. Volunteer gunners were wanted and Prince Sturdza, Comte de Pimodan and my brother were chosen; they were accompanied by a few gendarmes and two or three American Albanians, who acted as interpreters and made themselves very useful. When the necessary preparations were completed, this "battery" left for Alessio on an Italian tramp steamer.

During the first half of June there was only one incident worth noting, which, though it seems unimportant enough now, was very serious to us and almost caused very grave complications. This is what happened: as was mentioned in the last chapter, a sort of secret police had been organised as the regular force, which we had inherited from the provisional government, the ruling power in Albania before the King's arrival, had proved absolutely incapable of fulfilling its functions. As a matter of fact the most useful thing that the regular police used to do, was to help foreigners with their luggage, on arriving at Durazzo, for which they of course received baksheesh. Our new police had for some weeks been watching the movements of certain foreigners and on the night of the 5th June they notified Colonel Thomson, the commandant of the town, that they had noticed lamp signals, which were being made from a house tenanted by Italians. At least one of these was suspected of being a spy, or anyway in the secret service of his government. The lamp signals were said to have been noticed three nights in succession and it was also asserted that answering signals had been made by the insurgents on the heights of Raspul. Certain Morse messages emanating from one of the windows in question were read by officers on the destroyers in the harbour, and from the reading it appears that some secret code was being used, though one message was sent in the Italo-Albanian dialect.

Captain Jan Fabius, the most reckless and dashing of the Dutch officers, together with several policemen and volunteers, surrounded the suspected house and without further ado arrested two of its occupants, both Italian subjects, regardless of the consequences. A third, who was with them, managed to get away through a window and make good his escape in the darkness without being recognised; as the whole town knew the trio in question, this third man's identity was an open secret. Owing to the Italian Minister's intervention, he was however not arrested and had the discretion to retire from Durazzo as soon as he could get away.[39]

Hardly had the arrest been affected and Colonel Thomson appeared on the scene, when Baron Aliotti and followers also arrived. The Italian Minister protested against the arrest, which had been carried out contrary to the Capitulation Laws,[40] which were still in force, but had apparently been forgotten by the authorities in the heat of the fray. The Colonel stood his ground and argued the matter out, claiming that some clause in the Capitulation Laws permitted immediate arrest in certain exceptional cases; he claimed that this was such a one and defended the conduct of his subordinate. Apparently the

Minister did not consider the Colonel's opinion on this point of very great importance and took an opposite point of view. The result was that a long and wordy debate ensued, to the great delight of the onlookers, who cheered on their respective champions noisily; the Italians shouted, the crowd shouted and the two opponents shouted, but finally the Colonel's voice rose above the din and the victory for the time being was his! In spite of the Italians' remonstrations, he insisted on searching the house and seizing his prisoners' correspondence, though he allowed his two captives to remain at large, on their minister's undertaking that they would not attempt to escape from Durazzo.

Unfortunately I was not present to witness this pleasant scene, so cannot guarantee the absolute truth of the details; however several independent witnesses all told me exactly the same story, so I daresay that the account that I have given is accurate enough.

This time the Italian Minister was really angry and demanded Thomson's instant dismissal, or a formal apology from him. During an "audience" he had with the Mbret on the subject, he raised his voice to such a pitch, that we could hear what he was saying right away in the Oriental Room, almost the other end of the house. He failed absolutely in his object, as the Colonel roundly refused to apologise; the wily Minister of Justice also said that the King could not possibly dismiss Thomson, as the Dutch Gendarmerie Mission had been appointed by the Concert of Europe. In such a serious matter the International Commission would have to be consulted and would have to decide the case, as it saw fit. This was a good point and gave the king time.

The Albanian Ministers and other officials begged Thomson to apologise, to avoid all further trouble, but he would not listen to them and maintained that he was in the right; they pointed out to him that he should do so for the King's sake, but the gallant Dutchman remained firm and only replied "Volontiers je donnerais ma vie au Roi, mais jamais mon honneur!". There were fifteen witnesses who were willing to swear that they had seen the signalling during the night in question, but in spite of such a lot of evidence, the case had to be dropped and the Italians escaped without any further molestation. From the foregoing pages it will be seen that, with the exception of this little incident, nothing of importance happened during the first half of June, though the air was heavy with suspicion and treason and everything was preparing for trouble. Every day brought its crop of sensational rumours and Durazzo, on the whole, was not a haven of rest for anybody, least of all for us at the palace!

Chapter Seventeen

. . . .

THE REBELS ATTACK DURAZZO

The 15th of June marked our one and only triumph over the rebels during the whole of the rebellion and even this one modest victory was nullified by the death of our gallant commandant, Colonel Thomson. At about four o'clock in the morning I woke up to find Turkhan Pasha shaking me violently by the shoulder; he was very excited and quite annoyed at finding me still asleep. "A fine soldier you are to be sleeping at such a time" he said; "Get up and to work! You don't appear to know that the insurgents have attacked the town in force and have established themselves in some of the outlying houses. It appears that they took the outposts by the Porta Romana by surprise and overwhelmed them before they could offer resistance; at dawn they made a general attack on our positions."

I heard the firing right enough now that I was properly awake and jumped into my clothes as quickly as possible. On looking out of the window, as I was dressing, I noticed a few stray bullets dropping on the square below, where they kicked up little clouds of dust. The King himself appeared at the door, as I was about to go to his room; he had been awakened by the firing and wanted to ride straight away to visit the defences. Turkhan Pasha joined me in persuading him not to do so for the present and to let me go out first and bring him Colonel

Thomson's report. As Ekrem Bey was not yet up, he could not have accompanied the King immediately anyway, so the Mbret gave way and sent me ahead. I ran down to the stables and getting a saddle onto one of our small native ponies, rode across the square and past the "douane" to our main position by the petroleum magazine.

First I kept close to the sea, intending to cut across the waste land, which stretches from here right up to the Tirana road; however I found the ground too swampy and as bullets were whizzing my way in a rather disconcerting manner, I turned round and rode out through the town, where I was under cover most of the way. The last three hundred yards or so I had to gallop along a straight bit of road, which ought to have been swept by the enemy's fire, but for some reason was not. At the magazine we had two big trenches on both sides of the road; they were manned by Mirdites and Kosovans, who were blazing away ammunition for all they were worth; on the left a couple of machine-guns were hammering away with monotonous regularity. Here I found Colonel Thomson, whom I asked how things were going; although he himself was standing in the open behind the row of trenches, he told me to clear out as I would get hit for a certainty. He told me to assure the King that the position was perfectly safe for the present, though a number of the insurgents had managed to get close to the trenches in the long grass.

Our people were firing so heavily that one could not hear the enemy's bullets and I therefore did not realise that there was much danger in staying here. As I thought that it would make a good impression on the men to see somebody from the palace, I rode along the line cheering; our "Rroft Mbreti!" quite drowned the "Allah il Allah!" (or words to that effect), with which the insurgents kept up their spirits, and our men were delighted. Then I turned to ride home; as I did so, a hail of bullets followed me, hitting the road, the hedges and, in fact everything except myself. I did not wait to see whether the rebels' aim would improve, but dug my spurs into the pony and galloped down the road for all I was worth, till, getting back to the houses, I was under cover again.

This was the first time I had been under fire, but though I am of a very nervous disposition, I felt absolutely no fear all the time. I had a choky feeling in the throat, due to the excitement of the moment, a sort of buck-fever (the scourge of the deer-stalker), that is all, but I never dreamed of the possibility of being hit. I was very much surprised at myself, as I had always been afraid that I would not be able to stand the strain if I got under fire, and turn tail at the critical moment.

On getting back to the palace, I found that the King, contrary to our arrangement, had already left with Ekrem Bey to visit the battery on the hill behind the barracks; so I had a hurried breakfast and set out again. This time I turned to the right by the doctor's house, now the Court Hospital, and over the swampy ground beyond; I thought that I knew this well enough, as I frequently came out here for an evening stroll; however I soon found that what would carry me, would not necessarily carry my pony! Suddenly the ground gave way under us and the pony sank up to its belly in the bog; I went in to nearly up to the knees, which was not at all pleasant, though not as dangerous as it seemed; smothered in mud we managed to scramble out safe and sound. From here I rode past the Italian brickfields and climbed the hill behind them; I chose this route, as every other was exposed to the enemy's fire and here at least we were more or less under cover. As the hill is very steep on this side and is devoid of any paths, I had to drag the pony most of the way. Close to the top of the hill, I noticed a gendarmerie detachment, which I immediately headed for; when I came up to it, I found that the men were thinking only of their personal safety and had taken up a safe position, from which they could neither see nor shoot at anything; their captain had been killed, apparently by a stray bullet, and I could not induce them to go forward either by threats or flattery. So I rode to the position they ought to have occupied a few yards higher up and, dismounting, had a look round through my field glasses. As I stood on the sky-line I must have made a good mark, but not a shot was fired at me, nor could I see any signs of the enemy; as soon as the bold gendarmes realised that there was now no danger in doing so, they decided to join me, though they had at first begged me not to do so myself! Carefully they crept forward, taking advantage of every fold of the ground; from this new position they got an extended field of fire; the rebels were supposed to be on the hill opposite, but I did not see anything of them and all remained silent. I left these heroic gendarmes, who had now started a steady fusillade into the air to keep up their spirits, and rode on; in a few minutes I came upon the extreme left of the main hill position, where some Malissori were firing hard in the direction of the enemy, though my personal belief is that they could not see anything to aim at; anyway I could not see a thing myself and our fire was not being returned. The Malissori told me that they were running out of ammunition, so, having seen enough for the present to satisfy me that there was no immediate danger in this quarter, I turned homeward, in order to have cartridges sent up from the store in the town. On the way I met the senior Dutch doctor and Baroness Godin[41], who had come up to look after the wounded; it was from them that I first heard of Colonel Thomson's death.

He had been hit in the jugular vein only a couple of minutes after I had left him and had died almost instantaneously. Though he was very popular among the natives, there was not one attempt to go to his assistance when he fell; Major Lucas Roelfsema and Mr. Arthur Moore, of the Times, ran forward under a heavy fire and brought him under cover. Moore was recommended for Dutch and Albanian decorations on account of his gallant conduct on this occasion.

Roelfsema was now the senior Dutch officer in Durazzo and took over command for the time being. After visiting the depot to get ammunition sent out to the Malissori, I returned to the palace to make my report. The King had not heard of Colonel Thomson's death and the news came as a great blow to him, as he had great confidence in his loyalty and ability. Everybody was at breakfast, so I joined in and had a second sound meal, for which I was quite ready. The King had only just returned from the battery, where he had had quite an exciting experience. Hardly had he arrived by the guns, when the insurgents made a sudden flank attack from the hills and poured bullets into the battery position; later I was told that the Mbret had behaved very creditably whilst under fire, but that Ekrem Bey, who was with him at the time, persuaded him to cut short his visit and return home, as he had no right to endanger his life. The impression made upon the people of Durazzo by the King's appearance amongst them in the hour of danger was excellent and he was cheered by high and low as he rode through the streets.

After a short rest I went out again to see what was happening beyond the barracks; at the foot of the hill, I left my pony with an old gendarme and climbed up on foot, making for the trenches, which had been dug on the top some days before. The fire here was heavy on our side and apparently fairly successful, as I saw quite a number of dead bodies in the valley below us, where the insurgents had tried to advance; the enemy answered our fire feebly and very few of our men were hit. I went from trench to trench along the whole line of our position, cheering the men on, till the whole valley resounded with "Rroft Mbreti". As there appeared to be no danger in this quarter, I returned to the hill over the barracks, where I sat down for a time to watch our gunners at work. This morning we had about six guns in action, and the shooting since the 23rd had improved considerably owing to the arrival of fresh volunteers, some of whom were reserve officers in the Austrian or German artillery. The best shooting was made by two guns over the barracks, which were run by an Austrian reserve officer, who had come to Albania as a civil engineer, Herr Hässler. I was with his battery, when he received the order to bombard a small guard house on the Tirana road, some three hundred yards in front of our swamp position; the first shot was a little high, the second rather under the mark and the third hit it and exploded properly. A whole crowd of insurgents, at least twenty of them who had taken cover in the house, now dashed out of it, running back towards their own lines for dear life. A couple of shrapnels were sent after them to keep them on the run and several of them were laid out before they could reach safety. Though I am not brutal on the whole, I must admit that these few well-placed shots gave me great pleasures. Later it was claimed that the man who shot Colonel Thomson, was in the house and an old Martini rifle found in the ruins, which was supposed to be the weapon which caused the Colonel's death, was presented to the King as a souvenir. The rifle was shown to visitors at the palace as a trophy and they were told the story solemnly, though I fail to see how it could be claimed that just this rifle was the one. Nobody saw from where the shot came that killed Thomson. As a matter of fact there were at first even rumours that he had been murdered by one of our own men (see Note 23 for a different interpretation of Thomson's death).

Chapter Eighteen

· · · ·

THE INSURGENTS REPULSED

After remaining for some time on the hill, I went down to the barracks, where there were some more guns, manned by Germans, and here also the shooting was quite satisfactory. I had been here for a few minutes, when we suddenly heard shells singing over our heads; one or two passed us and while we were still wondering where they came from, one of them exploded about fifty yards in front of us, on what we called the barrack-square, though in reality it was only the grassy slope of the hill. This sudden bombardment gave us rather a start, as we naturally enough presumed that the enemy was using one of the guns that they had taken from us and we knew that our gun position was entirely untenable against artillery fire. Some more shells passed over our heads without exploding and we then discovered that a gun had been taken over to the other side of the town by Captain Fabius and that he was now bombarding the hills on our left rear, where a strong party of the rebels had been sighted. As no further shells burst in our vicinity, we felt a good deal more comfortable!

On our left front I heard a machine-gun banging away and soon spotted it behind a hedge at the bottom of the hill; seeing a Dutch uniform by it, I decided to visit it and rode off along the road, which leads out of the town on this side and gradually disappears in the dried swamp or pasture land. By the last hut on the outskirts of the town, I tied up my pony, intending to go across the field on foot; however while I was having a last look round from here, before going out in the open, I saw our machine-gun detachment suddenly retire with their gun, as if the devil were behind them; at the same time the enemy, who had worked his way round the foot of the hill, opened a heavy fire on our men; they were also using a machine-gun, which however was not visible. After some minutes I spotted the insurgents' firing line behind a hedge and lining a sunken road, about three hundred yards in front of us; two or three Malissori were behind the house and I asked one of them to lend me his rifle for a minute; however he would not let me touch it, and nearly turned nasty, so I got on to my pony again and rode back towards the barracks. Hardly had I left the cover of the house and got back onto the road when the rebels caught sight of me and turned their fire in my direction; the air was thick with bullets and the little puffs of dust all round me showed me that this was not a safe place to remain in, so I had a second hard gallop back to safety. At the barracks I pointed out the insurgents' new position and had a couple of guns turned onto it; when I left, some minutes later the gunners were making such good practice with shrapnel that the enemy did not risk a further advance. As I found out later, the officer in charge of the machine-gun that I had set out to visit was Captain Sar, who, not having been able to see the rebel advance on account of the formation of the ground, had only just managed to retire in time to avoid being cut off.

By now the attack had been brought to a standstill all round and in places the enemy was beginning to retire, so I decided to return to the palace. I had however hardly got into the town proper, when there was a sharp crack, as of a rifle, within about twenty yards of me and a bullet whizzed past my ear. By the sound I judged that the shot had been fired out of a window, but I could not exactly locate from which one; there happened to be no passers-by on the road at the time and I did not see where the bullet hit. The incident gave me a start and bearing in mind all the warnings that I had received on the

23rd of May and afterwards, I decided that it would be wiser for me to trot through quiet, little frequented thoroughfares in future, if I wanted to avoid unpleasant experiences; I felt absolutely no desire to leave my bones in Albania!

The rest of the afternoon I had to stay at home, as there was a certain amount of work for me to do; proclamations and letters of thanks to the loyal chieftains had to be written and altogether my time was fully occupied. As I had seen the best part of the fight, I did not object to returning to my clerical duties for a few hours.

Our guns were kept busy till after 5 o'clock, pounding away at the retreating enemy, till he was out of range. The insurgents, once they had started their retirement, seemed to loose all discipline and cohesion, running away like a lot of frightened sheep, hardly daring to look behind them. After tea I went up to the guns again, in time to see the finish and then had food and wine sent to the weary gunners, who deserved the King's bounty after their hard day's work.

At about five o'clock there was a tremendous burst of rifle fire from the swamp positions, which lasted for the best part of quarter of an hour, and the guns also redoubled their efforts; of course it was at once rumoured in the town that the rebels had renewed their attack and this gave scaremongers the opportunity of creating a panic; however this time it turned out to be nothing but a touch of the comic. Two insurgents appear to have been left behind by their comrades when these evacuated their advanced positions, close to our line of trenches. Suddenly they jumped up from their hiding places in the long grass and, legging it for all they were worth, made for the swamps; they waded through them as best they could, up to the knees in the slime and water. Everybody opened fire on these unfortunate individuals, so that bullets and shrapnel lashed up the water all round them. Ten minutes it must have taken them to get across; just as they reached terra firma, one of them was hit and fell forward onto his face, one leg still in the water; we all felt sorry that he did not escape, as he deserved to do, after the ordeal he had gone through. Those two fugitives cost us at least twenty shells and certainly ten thousand cartridges; and with all this expenditure of ammunition we had only succeeded in bagging one of them!

The evening passed off peacefully enough and the naval doctors got to work on the wounded; they were assisted by several Austrian and German ladies, one or two of whom had shown the greatest bravery during the day, tending the wounded in the trenches quite regardless of their own safety.

Late at night there was an alarm and firing recommenced all along the line; it was however soon evident that the enemy had not attacked in force and had only fired a few shots to annoy us (as they frequently did from this time onward). Though we had no more fighting that night there was still a lot of work for us. At a late hour, the ship, which had been sent to Alessio early in the morning for reinforcements, arrived with about a thousand men from the north, under Major Henri Kroon, the Dutch officer commanding the Northern gendarmerie, who was to take Colonel Thomson's place as commandant of Durazzo. Von Trotha and I were kept busy superintending the debarkation and saw everybody safely landed. The men were then drawn up on three sides of the square and when all was ready, the King went out to inspect them; it was now about one o'clock - a rather unusual hour for a parade!

Our total losses during the day's fighting numbered some forty officers and men, while the rebels left double that number of dead on the field and their total losses were estimated at over two hundred men. However the loss of Colonel Thomson was more than deplorable, not only for his many friends, but for the whole of Albania; he had made a name for himself in the country and was without doubt the Mbret's ablest servant. It is very sad to think that such a man should have lost his life in so petty a cause! His body was transported from the Petroleum Magazine to a tent in the yard in front of the Court Hospital. Next day we temporarily buried him in the enclosure of the central karakul. The whole of Durazzo attended the funeral, the King walking behind the coffin, as chief mourner; the coffin was carried by gendarmes and the foreign warships sent detachments to escort it. A British naval chaplain from H.M.S. Defence read the funeral service; everybody of note was present and it was even rumoured that quite a number of the insurgents had come into the town to pay their last respects to this gallant Dutch gentleman.

The Defence had arrived at Durazzo that morning and Admiral Troubridge[42] was welcomed with open arms; the presence of a British cruiser in the harbour gave us all a wonderful feeling of safety, as we knew that, as long as she remained with us, we would not suffer from a second episode like the one that we had experienced on the 23rd May. Who knows whether, if a British warship had been at Durazzo that day, the Albanian experiment might not have succeeded?

Admiral Troubridge was now the senior naval officer in the port; he often came on land, always accompanied by his flag lieutenant and an orderly and his burly figure, sunburnt face and snow white hair made a great impression on the simple native mind; the gipsies thought that he was some sort of potentate and looked upon him with great respect. When there was a night attack, the Admiral was usually to be found on shore and the presence of his armed boats did much to do away with panics in the town; we became great friends and he often looked me up in the evening to hear the local news and smoke a cigar in the palace garden, before retiring to his ship for the night.

Chapter Nineteen

. . . .

An Unsuccessful Sortie

The Durazzo garrison having won such a decided victory over the vastly superior numbers of the insurgents, the people of the town now thought that the position was saved and that the rebellion would fizzle out in the course of a few days. A council of war was held at the palace and it was decided to attack the rebels on the heights of Raspul and push them back to Tirana; it was hoped that they would not show fight, lay down their arms, and go home quietly. We felt particularly enterprising, as the reinforcements from the north must have brought our garrison to over three thousand men; the exact number I have forgotten. Unfortunately we did not know that the insurgents' spirit was quite unbroken, and that they had turned the heights of Raspul into a very strong fortified position; as no patrols were ever sent out and we did not credit the enemy with any military organisation, nobody knew that they had dug trenches all over the place, from which they were able to sweep the ground over which we would have to advance.

It was agreed that we were to make a sortie before sunrise on the 18th of June, advancing in perfect silence and awaiting dawn under the hill, close to where the rebels' front line was supposed to be; the enemy was to be taken by surprise and it was hoped that the attack would have an immediate and decisive result. The majority of our leaders felt quite assured of success though, as far as I can remember, Major Kroon, who had gained his military experience in the Dutch East Indies, was not as sanguine as the others, because he knew from experience how unreliable irregular troops are apt to prove themselves in an attack.

The plans were kept very dark, as it was feared that the rebels, who had many sympathisers in the town, might get wind of them and take precautionary measures to frustrate them. In fact our plans were kept so quiet that I had almost forgotten all about the scheme, when the valet woke me on the morning of the 18th with the intelligence that our main body had already left the town and that stragglers were streaming out on their way to Raspul.

It was about 8 o'clock, so, according to the book, the attack ought to have been over by now and the pursuit of the enemy in full swing; so I was more than surprised to hear that the battle had not even started. It was not till afterwards that we heard that the attack had started six hours late, owing to petty quarrels amongst the chieftains and the laziness of their men, who did not turn up in time at the appointed places of assembly. From my window I could see the Kosovans advancing along the seashore with a huge Albanian flag, which they planted some hundreds of yards beyond the bridge, in order to indicate their position to the artillery, which was to support them. This detachment, which was commanded by Isa Boletin, had the task of guarding our right flank against any surprise counter attack that might be made from the direction of Sasso Bianco and Kavaya. The remainder of our force, consisting mainly of Mirdites and Malissori, was sauntering out along the Tirana road in groups, talking and smoking as if going out for a day's holiday in the country. As the native chieftains did not like any interference from the Dutch gendarmerie officers and were under the impression that they knew all that there was to be known about fighting, no scouts or advance-guards had been sent ahead to reconnoitre the ground and locate the enemy's exact position.

As may be imagined, these slovenly methods courted

disaster; suddenly our men found themselves under heavy fire and, as they could not see from where it was coming, were unable to reply to it. There was a general stampede for cover, in the course of which several of our men got knocked over. As soon as order had been restored and the rebels' position ascertained, we returned the fire and the Mirdites gradually worked their way forward in open order. The artillery at Durazzo supported them, but, as the range was rather too far, the fire was not very effective; to remedy this, two guns were brought forward, one as far as the bridge and a second one some six hundred yards beyond it on the Tirana road.

The foreign volunteers tried to lead on the Mirdites, who now showed too much caution, and seven of them charged up the hill to within two or three hundred yards of the enemy's position, where they found some cover and had a rest; however the bold hillsmen would not follow them, so getting no support, they were reluctantly compelled to retire. It is worth mentioning that one of these volunteers, an Austrian reserve officer, had been shot through the shoulder during the night of the 15th and was carrying his arm in a sling; a very sporting effort, worthy of the highest praise!

During the first half of the morning, I was kept fully occupied indoors, so could not take part in the attack; however later on I again managed to get out and got more than my share of the fun! At about 11 o'clock, when our attack was at its height, the leader of the Mirdites, Marco Gioni, cantered back to the town and pulled up at the Ordnance Depot, where he asked for vaseline to be sent out to his men, who, he said, could not carry on without it, as their rifles were beginning to jam with the heat. There was no vaseline at the depot, so he continued his journey and finally fetched up at the palace, where we were all far too busy to see him. Tired by his long ride and the heat of the day, he retired to the nearest cafe to drink beer, a far more congenial occupation than fighting and one in which he excelled; he was a good Christian, was Marco, not a total abstainer like the poor Mahommedan insurgents, whom he despised!

Not so long afterwards, he returned to the palace again and asked for an audience as he had some very important news for the Mbret which wanted immediate attention. He told the King that he had received a message from one of his chiefs that a certain gendarmerie officer, Abdullah Effendi, who was in charge of the gun on the bridge, had turned traitor and was firing into our own men, who had already suffered considerable losses. Needless to relate, Abdullah Effendi was a Mahommedan; as a matter of fact he was one of the Dutchmen's most reliable and willing native subordinates and colleagues - one of the few that they had real confidence in. The King told me to go out and see what was happening and take any necessary steps, should Marco Gioni's report prove to be correct; of course I was only too pleased at the order, particularly as rather disquieting rumours were beginning to come in from the front. A messenger informed us, just as I was leaving, that our attack had come to a standstill and that we were barely holding our own at the foot of the hill; only now was it realised that the enemy had fortified himself and that his machine-guns made a frontal attack almost impossible!

So once again I mounted my little pony and rode out; en route I met crowds of reserves still leaving the town on their way to the fight and also a number of wounded and others, who had done enough fighting for the day and were going home to rest from their labours. With regret I noticed that by far the majority of the returning soldiers belonged to this latter category.

On the outskirts of the town a red-cross station had been rigged up by some Albanian doctors, who were assisted by foreigners and several of the educated townspeople; on this occasion a number of Italians were doing very good work among the wounded. As a matter of fact the Albanian Red Cross ought really to be called the Red Star, as this was the symbol adopted by the government, both the Cross and Crescent having been objected to by one section of the population or the other.

Taking cover behind the petroleum magazine I noticed Admiral Troubridge's flag-lieutenant, Bridgeman, and several others who had come out here as spectators. I galloped up the road, on both sides of which lay dead donkeys, killed by accident on the 15th, which, as the weather was very hot, did not tend to improve the atmosphere. By the bridge I found Abdullah Effendi and for some minutes watched him at work. He was not firing at the Mirdites, as had been stated by Marco Gioni, and to me it appeared that his aim was, if anything, just as accurate as that of the foreign volunteers; he set his fuses correctly and his shells burst in the right place. As other reliable people were with him, I felt perfectly satisfied that the charge brought against him was unfounded. Perhaps it had only been made because Marco Gioni, as a good Christian, mistrusted everybody that did not share his own religious beliefs.

As I was about to return home, to tell the King that everything appeared to be in order, Isa Boletin came cantering up from the front and shouted something to us in Albanian; what he said was interpreted to me by the gendarme officer now holding the bridge, who spoke a few words of French. He asked that somebody should be sent out to the advanced gun and have it brought back immediately, as the insurgents had made a determined attack on our left flank and were driving back the Kosovans. A mounted gendarme, who happened to be on the spot showed no inclination to ride out as his horse was tired, so I undertook the job myself.

Chapter Twenty

. . . .

A Decisive Defeat

From the bridge onward the road leading across the swamps is raised a couple of yards above the general level of the surrounding land; on the right of it, looking towards Raspul, there are a number of low mounds of sand, overgrown with long, coarse grass and grey-green reeds. On the outward journey I saw the Kosovans, who were holding this broken ground and formed a sort of protecting screen for this, our only line of communication; they only got up for a moment to fire and then lay down again under cover. What they were shooting at, I could not see, but the bullets, which continually buzzed over showed that a hidden enemy was returning the fire. Occasionally a man ran back and took cover behind the embankment on which the road was built, opening fire again over the heads of his comrades in front. Further on I met crowds of Mirdites, who were streaming back from the left and centre of our position; some of them were wounded, but the great majority of them were running like two year olds, or frightened sheep, hardly daring to look behind them. To prove their loyalty to the Mbret, they muttered "Rroft Mbreti", as they passed me, but nothing on earth would induce them to go back to the fight! When I arrived at my destination, I found Major Kroon with half a dozen German and Austrian volunteers, who were working their gun quite calmly, though the insurgents were now not more than three or four hundred yards away and had opened fire on them just before my arrival. I delivered Isa Boletin's message to Major Kroon, who ordered an immediate retreat; it took the amateur gunners some time to take their gun to pieces, pack it onto ponies and save the ammunition; however they managed to get back to the bridge without loss, though the rebels had by that time come up so close that they had to keep them at bay with their automatic pistols. (This may be slightly exaggerated as my informant, though a very plucky soldier, was of rather an imaginative turn of mind.)

As soon as the message had been delivered, I galloped back to the bridge; this was not exactly pleasant, as the rebels, having driven back the Kosovans from their advanced positions, now gave me a very warm time at pretty close range. They were advancing in skirmishing order among the sand-hills and blazed away at me for all they were worth; they were not much over a hundred yards from the road, but thanks to their extraordinarily inaccurate shooting I got through all right to the bridge. It seems almost like a miracle that the gun-team, which followed me some minutes later, did not lose any men or ponies! At the bridge, to which the Kosovans had fallen back, I told Isa Boletin that his message had been delivered and that the gun was on its way back; from here I galloped back to the barracks, where I pointed out the insurgents' new position to the gunners. They did not know that the rebels had advanced on the right, as the Kosovans, when they retired, forgot to bring the flag with them; so the gunners naturally enough thought that our people were still holding the advanced positions and that everything was in order. As a matter of fact the rebels were now round our flag; we opened fire on them with our guns and very soon saw that the fire was effective.

I think that it was partly due to our fire that the rebels did not annihilate our retreating force, now a dejected crowd of fugitives. The insurgents had made acquaintance with our artillery on the 15th, and did not attempt to advance after we had got the guns to play on them.

I returned to the palace and reported everything to the King, who, on hearing of the Mirdites retirement, sent out Selim Bey Wassa to try and stop the rout. Selim was sent in preference to anyone else as he was supposed to have a certain amount of prestige among the tribesmen, as his family claimed descent from the powerful Kastrati clan;[43] as he was a thorough sportsman, he was delighted at this chance of distinguishing himself and I am certain did his best to turn the tide. However he could do nothing with the Mirdites, who made every sort of feeble excuse for running away and continued to run till they were well inside our second line of defences; they were thoroughly downhearted, but promised Selim that they would return to the fight later in the day, after they had had some refreshment and rest.

I changed ponies and rode round the hill positions to see that all was in order there, in case of our being counter-attacked in the rear; to my great astonishment, I found many of our trenches quite empty and altogether not one quarter of the officers or men at their posts. I hurried back to the town and got hold of the Bishop of Alessio, who had more influence than anybody else over the northern mountaineers and asked him to help me get the men back to the trenches. He got to work with a will and by coaxing and cursing them alternately, he succeeded in getting his turbulent tribesmen to return to the sectors that had been allotted to them. This, too, was only just done in time, as when I was doing a second round of those position, to make certain that the Bishop's exhortations had born fruit, the insurgents attacked us from the hills beyond.

There was a heavy fusillade along the whole line and, as our trenches were now fully manned, the attack was easily repulsed. The losses were practically nil in this quarter and I do not believe that we inflicted any serious losses on the enemy. Probably this attack was only meant to annoy us and the insurgents may have had no intention of pushing it home; still it was a good thing they found us well prepared to receive them!

As I got back to the town some Italians came rushing in from the brickfields, close to the sea; they appeared to be panic-stricken and kept shouting that thousands of rebels were congregated on the hills where I had just been, and were coming into the town. As I knew that there was no truth in this, I gave the noble workers a piece of my mind and threatened them with the most terrible penalties, should they attempt to spread their lie in the town. In spite of my threats, they or some other evil-disposed persons managed to spread rumours of all sorts, for which there was no sort of foundation, as the better elements amongst the garrison had taken up their defensive positions again and were keeping off the rebels. On account of the guns the enemy did not make a serious counter-attack from the swamp side, as I have already mentioned, so our position was quite safe! The right practically came to a standstill soon after midday, as the rebels remained fairly inactive and our men were too disheartened to attack them a second time.

It was never discovered what caused the panic amongst the Mirdites in the morning, just as they were on the point of succeeding in the attack. They explained that they had been told, by whom they could not say, that we had been surprised by the rebels in the rear and that the town was in danger of falling into their hands. Another story was that the Mahommedan soldiers, left behind at Durazzo, had mutinied and were attacking the palace, as the foreign guard had been withdrawn. The attack in our rear only took place some time after the stampede of the Mirdites, as has already been shown, and the other rumour was equally unfounded, the Mahommedans having behaved fairly well throughout; as a matter of fact it was thanks to them that the Mirdites managed to make good their escape. Who started all these rumours was never found out, but it seems certain that they were spread for a purpose and succeeded in causing a senseless panic at a critical moment, when cool heads might have succeeded in taking the insurgents' trenches. The Austrian party in the town naturally enough took this opportunity of laying the blame on the Italians, who were always suspected of intriguing with the rebels and were consequently cordially disliked by the loyalists.

The end of it all was that Marco Gioni suddenly found himself very unpopular, not only with the government, but also with his own men, some of whom threatened to punish him "for his treason". The Mirdites laid the blame for their defeat to his incapacity as a leader and also claimed that he had not paid them the money that had been promised them by the government. As we did not want to have a murder committed, it was found advisable to send him home on leave; in fact I never saw his face again!

In the afternoon the insurgents gradually retired to their entrenched position on the hill and we pursued them with artillery fire till they were out of effective range. The British and Italian naval doctors rigged up hospitals, the former taking possession of a mosque, while the latter installed themselves in the Italian school; splendid work was done at both hospitals and the population has every reason to be grateful to the untiring zeal of the parties concerned. The Austrians at the Court Hospital continued their good work there and worked in perfect harmony with their foreign colleagues, with whom they were on the best of terms. The French, German and Russian ships' doctors also offered their services, which were however not accepted, as we had enough medical assistance without them.

During the day we lost at least one hundred and fifty men, killed and wounded, but this estimate is probably below the mark; all our hospitals were kept busy for some time afterwards and between sixty and eighty dead were buried in a heap beyond the bridge. Unfortunately they were badly buried and at night the foxes got at them, scraping away the earth; the result was most unpleasant for anybody passing that way; as the spot was between our own lines and the insurgents', only parliamentaries had to pass it. The insurgents' losses were probably much lighter than our own, as their trenches protected them when we attacked, and their retreat was so orderly that our artillery did them comparatively little damage. They left very few dead on the field, as far as we know, and only about half a dozen wounded, who were brought in to Durazzo on stretchers, or by carriage. Among these wounded who fell into our hands was a Mahommedan priest from Shjak, who turned out to be a person of some importance and one of the local leaders of the revolution. He was brought to the Court Hospital in a dying condition, but the skill of the doctors saved his life and he remained there strongly guarded till the feast of Ramadan, when the King released him and gave him a free pardon. It was an eyesore to me to see his cunning face leering out of the hospital window, as I would like to have seen him hanged as a traitor, as he had deserved! However I daresay that the King's policy of trying to put him on his honour was the better.

Our defeat was decisive and everybody knew it; we were disheartened and felt that the insurgents were one too many for us. One thing is certain and that is that for the remainder of our stay at Durazzo we were practically prisoners there, and that it was unsafe to walk much further than our own trenches. For the ladies this was particularly annoying, but they took it philosophically; altogether they showed just as much courage as the men - if not more!

It gives me pleasure to relate that the only person in the house whom nothing could move was the English butler, who remained dignified whatever happened. One day when rumours were current that the rebels had got into the town and the guns on the hill had opened fire on them, I met the butler in the passage. He stopped me and asked me whether I had heard the news. "They tell me the rebels have got into the town!" He was sick of the continual shooting and panic, so added "Well, I don't care, let 'em come if they want to, but these scares do delay dinner so!"

Chapter Twenty-One

. . . .

An Armistice Arranged

After our lesson of the 18th, we did not undertake any fresh military adventures for a few days; however the insurgents would not leave us in peace and used to let off a few rounds at us after dark, to which our men regularly replied with a fearful fusillade, which cost the government a heap of money, without helping us in any way. About the only thing that was hit during these noisy battles was the air; on one occasion only did we succeed in hitting a donkey, though I believe he too belonged to our side!

On the 20th of June I happened to go over to the Austrian legation for tea; looking across the swamps from its spacious balcony, I saw a carriage with a white flag on it and a whole crowd of people collected round it on the Tirana road, by the heights of Raspul. I could not imagine what this assembly signified, so sent out a servant to try and find out about it in the town. He soon returned with the information that a deputation had been sent out from the town to treat with the rebels and try to arrange an armistice with them. As I had heard nothing about this deputation's being sent out, I went home immediately and reported the matter to the King; he had only just been told it by Akif Pasha, when it was already too late to stop it. The King was much annoyed at so important a step having been taken without his consent, but as Akif Pasha, now

Minister of the Interior, in whose loyalty he had absolute confidence, had given his support to it, he did not view it with alarm.

I begged the King to have nothing to do with it, as to me it seemed cowardly and wrong to conclude any sort of armistice, which would only be local and would enable the insurgents to throw their forces against Prenk Bib Doda's army, which was now supposed to be but two days march from Shjak. It must be remembered that we had no direct means of communicating with any of our armies, so that they would advance and attack the rebels during the truce; this would have instituted a serious breach not only of European, but also of native morals and would have had the most serious consequences. How a man like the King, trained as a soldier, an officer in the German army, could not see what a cowardly and despicable thing we were proposing to do, I fail to understand.

Of course the ministers and certain others, who preferred their creature comforts to their honour, may have brought forward plausible arguments to get the King's consent; but still, he ought never to have given in to them! I did my best to convince him, but failed. Von Trotha did not take the slightest interest, as he had long ago given up all hope; his one and only ambition was to get out of Durazzo without sullying his honour. Time after time he used to tell me that the King ought to go before he was removed by force, as he had proved himself quite unfit for his post. Poor von Trotha, who, as I have already mentioned, was an honourable and rather quick-tempered martinet, could not stand the continual shilly-shally which characterised the Albanian government. Of politics he may have understood very little, but this armistice he felt as a jab at his honour and he was so furious about it that he walked about like a bear with a sore head for days afterwards.

A forty-eight hours truce was arranged, which was sufficient to enable the insurgents to make their preparations to meet our northern armies, while they were safe from attack in front of Durazzo. It was only Prenk's caution (or was it his trickery?) which saved his army from absolute disaster. The

Dutch officers, from whom the negotiations had been kept
secret, were naturally enough besides themselves with
indignation and wanted to resign "en bloc"; they were disgusted
at the whole affair and absolutely sick of Albania, as they were
never given a fair chance of showing their worth and were
always left in the dark about everything until the last moment.
Major Kroon, who was a very solid, level-headed man,
managed to quiet his subordinates down again, as he saw how
disastrous their resignation would be to the country's welfare
and he wanted them to stay at their posts, whatever happened,
for the honour of their country.

On the 22nd of June, Coronation Day, the British colony
at Durazzo, consisting of about three people, went to lunch on
board the "Defence" with Admiral Troubridge. One of our
number was Miss Durham,[44] who had come to Durazzo from the
northern mountains, to help in nursing the wounded at the
British hospital. Except when I got away to a ship for a few
hours, I was practically always in harness and liable to be called
away at a moment's notice. Everywhere I went I kept my eyes
and ears open, in order to be able to help the King, to whom I
was still very much attached. Even while I was dressing, people
used to come and see me about all sorts of things, the majority
of which did not really concern me at all, and once or twice I
had to get up out of bed at night and work even during sleeping
hours.

For instance on the morning of the 23rd I was woken up at
2.45 a.m. by the Kavass, about an hour after I had turned in. He
announced the arrival of Monsieur Gurakuchi, Under-secretary
for Education,[45] and the Comte de Pimodan, both just returned
from Slinza, a coastal town about 25 miles north of Durazzo,
the northern army's new base, with important messages from
Prenk Bib Doda. We had had no news from the north for
several days, so I had them brought to my room. I found that
they wanted to return to Slinza early next morning, so I had to
wake up the King and send for Major Kroon, whose presence
was absolutely necessary. Plans were discussed and orders
written till about half past five, when our visitors left us and we

again retired to bed for a few hours rest. As I found it hopeless trying to get to sleep with the sun streaming in through the windows, I got up and went for a good long ride before breakfast, visiting all our trenches on the way.

Two days later the armistice was prolonged; this was much criticised, not only by the old objectors but also by Monsieur Nogga, the Finance Minister, who had just returned from a visit to Prenk's army, which he considered was quite strong enough to advance further and tackle the insurgents. Nogga was the one man in the cabinet who knew what he wanted and really worked, but he certainly was untiring in his efforts to help the Mbret through his difficulties. Without him nothing would ever have been done at all! He was here, there and everywhere, doing everybody's work for them; of course, when things went wrong, he was blamed for everything. Had there only been several Noggas in the cabinet, we might have done better!

On the 25th there was a stir in the town, as it was noticed that the insurgents had dug a new trench this side of Sasso Bianco and people swore that they could see a gun in it. As I had long ago given up believing anything I heard, I went out myself to see what truth there was in this; first to the advanced position by the bridge and then back to the battery, but, though my glasses were about the best in the town, I failed to see any signs of a gun in the new trench or anywhere near it. I tried to convince people that there was nothing to be alarmed about, but in spite of my efforts, everybody expected the town to be bombarded during the night.

That evening the Queen's youngest brother, Prince Gunther Schönburg-Waldenburg(1887-1960[46]), arrived by the Austrian Lloyd steamer Baron Bruck. After the others had gone to bed, I stayed up with him till daybreak, explaining the situation to him according to my point of view, and I think that he sympathised with me. As he was such a close relative, I could speak openly to him about matters, which could not be discussed with an outsider, and asked him to point out to the King some of the things, which could be remedied; things that only a member of the family could point out without giving offence.

The rebels now expressed their desire to negotiate "with a British officer", so Colonel Phillips,[47] in so-called command of the international force based on Scutari, who happened to be at Durazzo on a flying visit from Scutari, went over to Shjak. The rebels were barely courteous to him and so unreasonable in their demands, making a Mahommedan Prince a "sine qua non", that nothing came of this conference and Colonel Phillips returned, disgusted.

One evening I went to dinner on board the German cruiser Breslau, which escaped from the Adriatic at the beginning of the war, fled into the Dardanelles and was then added to the Turkish navy under the name of Midilli. Here I met several officers from the Defence, and none of us thought that a short six weeks would see us all tearing at each others' throats! It is worth mentioning that the British and German naval officers seemed to get on better with each other than they did with anyone else and one frequently saw them about together, the best of good friends.

The hot weather, as well as the continual work and worry, were now beginning to tell on everyone's nerves and tempers, so that quarrels and differences of opinion became of frequent occurrence. I myself was in anything but a tranquil frame of mind, as I knew that my brother was walking into the insurgents' trap with Prenk Bib Doda's army. To my great relief he turned up safe and sound on the 30th June, after an absence of nearly a month, and I was proud of him, when I found that his name was on the top of three lists of recommendations for a reward for his services.

Chapter Twenty-Two

. . . .

PRENK BIB DODA PASHA'S ARTILLERY

As was mentioned in an earlier chapter, Prenk Bib Doda's army was first assembled at Alessio and was to march on Shjak and Tirana from the north, thus freeing Durazzo. It will also be remembered that three Europeans had been sent up to support his army with a mountain gun. Arrived at Alessio, the gunners found Prenk's forces assembled in and around the town, doing nothing in particular. Major Kroon was at this time trying to put some sort of order into the bands of irregulars, of which the army was composed, and making preparations for an early advance. At Alessio the water supply was very inadequate, the climate feverish and altogether the place was not suited for a military camp; there was a good deal of sickness among the troops and sanitary arrangements there were non-existent.

Unfortunately an early start was out of the question as, although large quantities of supplies had been bought by the government, none had as yet arrived and there was even a shortage of arms and ammunition. The volunteers were furious at the delay and at the lack of organisation that they found. Matters became worse when Major Kroon was called to Durazzo, on the death of Colonel Thomson, and an Albanian officer, Shefket Bey, took his place.

As my brother did not care about sitting still, kicking his heels, he set to work to recruit some Mirdites and train them as artillerymen; he picked out twenty-five men who appeared suitable and started work by making them give him their "besa" (i.e. their oath to serve under him loyally). He would only take them under this stipulation, as he wanted to have his men well in hand and an Albanian very rarely goes back on his word of honour. He found the men very intelligent and quick to learn, but had the greatest difficulty in teaching them the most elementary form of discipline. For instance they failed to see why they should not smoke on parade, salute or do the ordinary gun-drill. In spite of their unruly ways, my brother did wonders with them, which is much to his credit as he had never served in the army, his only military experience having been gained in the band of the Eton volunteers.

At last the day for the general advance arrived and the army left Alessio in high spirits; it was probably about 2,500 strong, large numbers of the Mirdites who had become tired of waiting having deserted. To the great dismay of the gunners, the army only advanced at the rate of barely five kilometres a day and already bands of Malissori were detaching themselves from the main body to maraud the villages that lay on the line of march.

The gun was looked upon as a sort of fetish and had to be kept well in front in order to terrify any enemy that might be met. My brother's eyeglass was also a mysterious thing of awe, nobody being quite certain as to whether it was a part of the gun or connected with black magic; so to be on the safe side, the "English officer" was treated by everybody with the greatest respect. It may be that this respect was also partly due to the fact that my brother could lift parts of the gun, which any two of the natives found difficult to manage. Though the Albanians are such a well set up, hardy race, they appear to be physically weak, particularly in the arms; all the hard work at Durazzo was done by the gipsies, who are puny to look at, but can carry enormous weights on their shoulders.

After two or three days' march they reached Ishmi, about 20 miles north of Durazzo, and the same distance to the south of Alessio; a small market town, lying on a hill from which there is a splendid view of the surrounding country. The town is built round an old citadel. It had been reported that the rebels were holding this position in force, so a few shots were fired with the gun and our army advanced in open order, keeping up a searching fire, which was feebly returned by a few isolated rebels, who however retired before the approach of such an imposing host. Here my brother had some trouble with one of the over-cautious leaders who wanted him to open fire on a group, which my brother had watched for some time and knew to belong to our main body. Sturdza had applied to his minister for a few days leave, but his undiplomatic activities were discovered, and he was recalled and severely reprimanded. About this time Prince Sturdza was recalled to Bucharest and de Pimodan, acting as messenger between Durazzo and Prenk's army, my brother was left alone with the gun. A German commercial traveller who had done good work at Durazzo in all three fights but had now made his presence there undesirable, and an Austrian ex-soldier, were now sent up to help him.

Some days after their arrival, scouts reported that the insurgents had been discovered at a place called Malkuts, where they had taken up a strong position in an old tower, overlooking the valley. The gun was sent forward to bombard them and smash up the tower; the former could not be done, as there were no rebels to be seen, but the tower was destroyed. Thirteen shots were fired at it at three and a half kilometres and of these nine hit it; quite a successful morning's work for a person who had never fired off a gun before! The infantry did not go to inspect the damage done, as it was possible that some rebels might still have been hanging round the scene of the bombardment. In fact, it was not quite safe, so no more was done and the gun was taken back to Ishmi, where the victory was celebrated by the rest of the army. Unfortunately, it turned out that Malkuts was a friendly village and that the shelling of their tower had naturally hurt their feelings.

One evening there was some firing between the opposing outposts and the rumour immediately went round that the enemy was advancing in force and that the camp would be attacked during the night. At a late hour there was some more firing, but nobody seems to have actually seen any insurgents at all! However the unpleasant rumours were quite enough to terrify Prenk's gallant army, which had by now dwindled to seven hundred fighting men, as "all the rest had gone to drive the cattle"; this good old custom is still kept up among the Albanian mountaineers and plays by far the most important part in the native warfare. There was a general stampede and by midnight the gunners, who had not received any instructions, and knew nothing of an impending retirement, found themselves left to their own devices. There was nothing for it but to clear out as quickly as possible, and this they did without any undue delay.

So the three Europeans and the twenty-five Mirdite gunners who, having given their besa, had so far remained loyal to my brother up-saddled and trekked through the night. On the way they saw no signs of the rebels, though it was of course nervous work going through the enemy's country without a proper escort. It was a dark night and in fording a river, they lost a pony in the quicksand; this was their only misadventure and next morning they arrived at Slinza, where they found the gallant army assembled once more and full of beans.

My brother was by this time heartily sick of the Albanian methods of fighting and, as he was more than suspicious about the bona fides of the whole expedition, he made up his mind to return to Durazzo with his gun, fearing this might be taken from him by force. He was going to get this on board a rowing-boat, when a chieftain came up and stopped him from doing so. My brother told him that he was taking the gun back to the Mbret, to whom it belonged, but the old warrior only became threatening in his manner and answered "We'll see who the gun belongs to!". As it was no use arguing with him my brother went to Prenk Pasha in order to get his assistance. Prenk received him courteously, as always, but informed him that he would not be able to leave, as the insurgents had occupied some flats commanding the mouth of the river and would certainly not allow him to pass through. As my brother had seen some of

Prenk Bib Doda's boats, loaded with ammunition, going down the river without being in any way molested, he disregarded the yarn about the rebels and told the Pasha that he wished to leave instantly and would not mind taking the risk of having to run the gauntlet. So, much against his will, Prenk had to agree and give him his support; no further obstacles were put in his way and he in due course got his gun on board a small sailing vessel. Five of his Mirdites accompanied him, while the remainder of them were left behind with the ponies, as these had to be taken round to Alessio and from there to San Giovanni di Medua, whence they were shipped some days later on an Italian steamer. When they had got the boat into mid-stream, the Mirdites suddenly decided that they were too tired after their night march to do any rowing, no doubt considered infra-dig by the clansmen. My brother did not attempt to argue with them, but jumped out of the boat and, wading in the water up to his armpits, pulled it along behind him with a rope. This move had the desired effect, as the Mirdites, thoroughly ashamed of themselves, asked him to get back into the boat and, taking up their oars, gave him no further trouble. At the mouth of the river, they found the government steamer Herzegovina and returned to Durazzo on her.

For the remainder of my brother's stay in Albania, his Mirdites followed him about like faithful hounds and when he left for England they came to the landing-stage to see him off, and asked him to appoint their commander until he returned, which, they hoped, would be before the next battle. Though my brother did not give these fellows either presents or extra pay, their loyalty to him was really genuine, and when he left they transferred their allegiance to myself. Those simple brigands were not as bad as they were painted, and certainly far better than the half Turkish middle classes of the towns, who think that they are civilised because they know a smattering of one of the Western languages and have learned both oriental and European vices! I liked the brigands!

Chapter Twenty-Three

THE KING'S POWER BROKEN

It has already been touched upon in a former chapter that the government formed a plan to surround the rebels and force them to surrender; we accompanied the northern army commanded by Prenk Bib Doda in the last chapter, up to its arrival at Slinza. After this no more was heard of it as an attacking force and it retreated gradually towards the north. The enemy harried it and, as far as I can remember, the town of Alessio, which was almost entirely Roman Catholic and a loyalist stronghold, was for some time in danger of falling into the insurgents' hands.

A detachment of volunteers which had come from Scutari, now left Prenk's army, as everybody was fed up with his incapacity as a general. Some of these Scutarins came down to Durazzo, where they were welcomed with open arms and, being mostly better educated men than our local talent in central Albania, were given the opportunity of making themselves useful in the police.

The remainder of Prenk's army, after reinforcements had been sent to the capital, dispersed, a few small detachments being left on guard, in case the rebels should have attempted to attack the Mirdita. The Pasha himself came to Durazzo where he was needed by the King on account of his influence with the Mirdites, who were not always easy to handle and occasionally threatened to leave us "en masse".

We must now see what happened to the other armies, of which such great deeds had been expected; their shameful tale is quickly told. The north eastern army, under young Ahmed Bey Mati (later King Zog), consisting of about 2,000 Mahommedan Matians, at first advanced rapidly from its mountains without meeting with any resistance from the enemy and occupied the ancient hill-capital of Albania, Kruja. Ahmed Bey took the town by surprise and, as far as I remember, without having to fire a shot; later he again evacuated it, but it is not quite clear whether this step was really necessary or only a political manoeuvre. The army advanced on Tirana, occupied a strong position overlooking the whole Tirana valley and sat tight there. No attempt was made to attack the insurgents and the Matians remained inactive for some time, while their leader tried to come to terms with the enemy and occupy the town without any bloodshed. The story went round that the insurgents offered to make Ahmed Bey President of their proposed Central Albanian Republic, if he would come over to their side, but that he absolutely declined to consider the proposal, as he had given his besa to the Mbret and did not intend breaking his word. This north-eastern army cost the government a lot of money, which was wasted as it did nothing all the time. After a few weeks of waiting, it retired to its mountain fastnesses, taking with it all the rifles and ammunition which had been served out to it by the King's government. Public opinion at Durazzo charged Ahmed Bey with treason and certainly his conduct did appear rather curious; however I personally believe that the explanation he gave was perfectly plausible, and that was that his forces had been so weakened by desertion that he did not feel strong enough to attack the insurgents' headquarters. His men mostly sympathised with the rebels, the Matians being the most fanatical Mahommedans in the country, so it is not surprising that they deserted whenever they got the chance to do so. As Ahmed Bey, too, was a very strict Moslem, it is greatly to his credit that he remained at least outwardly loyal to the throne.

The eastern forces, consisting partly of regular gendarmerie, were beaten in one or two minor engagements and driven back towards Elbasan, which the insurgents succeeded in taking by a coup de main. Here two Dutch officers fell into the enemy's hands and when I left Albania, they had not yet been released.[48] So the eastern army disappeared from the scene of action having achieved nothing; part of it even changed sides and helped the insurgents actively!

The southern main army advanced from Valona; it consisted chiefly of Laps,[49] the greatest plunderers in Albania; this force marched through the Busekie (? Muzakia), a rich agricultural district inhabited by friendly people, stealing everything that came in its way. After bombarding a small rebel position with a mountain gun and advancing up to the Semeni river, the army was itself attacked by the enemy, who had waited for a chance when it was split up into marauding bands. The royal forces were taken entirely by surprise and after losing the artillery and a large number of killed and wounded retired to Valona by the shortest route. The peasants, whose villages they had pillaged during the advance, now rose in their rear and punished them during the retreat, throwing in their lot with the regular rebels, though they really had nothing in common with them. Valona itself was threatened for some time, but the rebels took no serious steps to take it as they probably knew that Italy would not permit them to occupy the town. So the southern main army also disappears from the scene as an attacking force; it remained in and round Valona for some time and in August sent some detachments to reinforce the garrison of Durazzo.

The second southern army, which was supposed to advance from Berat, did not get very far and sat tight. Its leader, Aziz Pasha Vrioni, who had been in the first cabinet as Minister for Agriculture and Commerce, was mishandled and narrowly escaped being shot by his own men. His army was in a state of anarchy and the various elements of which it was composed started fighting amongst themselves; some went over to the enemy, others tried to advance, but the majority ran back to

Berat, closely followed by the insurgents. At Berat, where some reinforcements had arrived from the south, a determined stand was made; during the defence of the town some old British ships' guns, presented by Lord Nelson to the 'Lion of Janina',[50] were used from the citadel. They were loaded with black powder and antique stone cannon balls, wrapped up in newspapers; they made a terrible noise, which gave confidence to the garrison, though it must be supposed that they did no great harm to the enemy. As far as I remember, Berat was taken by the rebels after pretty severe fighting and the remnants of the garrison, amongst whom were Captain Ghilardi and Mr. Spencer (see Notes 21 and 22), managed to make good their escape.

The insurgents swept everything before them, right down to Koritza, where the remnants of the Berat garrison helped to strengthen the loyalist forces; here they had one or two guns to support them. A determined stand was made and the insurgents were twice repulsed with heavy losses. Furious at their failure, they called upon the Epirotes to assist them, promising to hand over the town to them. A third combined attack was made and the enemy being now far too strong, the town was forced to capitulate. Part of the garrison got away in time to avoid surrender and thanks to Ghilardi and the American, Spencer, the guns and machine guns were saved; these two with a band of southern volunteers made their way back to Valona with the artillery intact. This was a very fine achievement, as their way ran through the enemy's country and they had to fight their way through the insurgents before they got back to civilisation. The Dutch officer, who had been at Koritza with them, got back to Valona some days earlier. The two volunteers complained bitterly about the underhand manner in which he had left them in the lurch, stating that he had changed into plain clothes and made his escape at night, without telling his companions anything about his intention. What truth there was in these assertions, I am not in a position to judge, as no questions were asked and in Albania charges were so often made, which on closer investigation, could not in any way be substantiated.

The foregoing account of the central Albanian campaign, which was spread over three months, June, July and August, is unfortunately very inaccurate, as reliable news was very scarce at Durazzo and most of our information came through more or less irresponsible adventurers and bandits, some of whom, I feel certain, allowed their imaginations to run wild. According to some reports our armies consisted of unlucky heroes, and according to others only the scum of the people was on the King's side and only fought for pay. I don't suppose we ever heard the truth and nothing but the truth! So the reader of this must be content with the few scraps of information that I am able to bring him, which however are quite sufficient to show that the King's forces were defeated all round by the insurgents, who throughout showed themselves far better soldiers than our own people. Of course this last is probably due to the fact that, being good Mahommedans, the majority of them had done their military service in the Turkish army and had learnt how to fight in the Balkan War. It also seems certain that they were led by Turkish and other Balkan officers, who understood the Albanian character better than our own Dutchmen and volunteers, most of whom came from northern Europe. When Austria declared war against Serbia, we heard that about twenty Serbian officers, who had been fighting against us, returned to their own country.

Our whole plans failed utterly and absolutely, but, whatever else can be said against the Mbret and his government, neither can be blamed for this failure, which was mainly caused by treason, bad discipline in the irregular armies and the incapacity of the native leaders. Altogether we must have had about 10,000 men in the field for a few weeks - sometimes more and sometimes less. What the insurgents put against us, we never found out, though it was estimated that they had about 15,000 men under arms during July and August. When they attacked Durazzo in June, they are supposed to have had 5,000 men round the town, but my personal belief is that all the figures given are much exaggerated. As we had quite a number of guns and machine guns and the rebels had no artillery at all to start with, we ought to have put down the insurrection easily and our defeat was not only defeat, but absolute disgrace!

The account of our military operations would not be complete without a brief mention of the Royal Albanian Navy; as everything else in the Six Month Kingdom, its career was short and inglorious. When the government decided to put down the insurrection and made its military preparations in the north, south, east and west, it also chartered a small steamer from an Austrian shipping company, the Herzegovina, which was at first only used as a transport. After a time a mountain gun was taken on board and mounted in the bow; there was great competition among the volunteers as to who should get the post of naval gunnery officer and several of them claimed the newly created post; it was finally given to Herr Hassler, whom we knew as a reliable man. One day the "fleet" put to sea with orders to bombard Kavaya; this it did and the experiment was repeated on several further occasions, though it is believed that practically no damage was done to the town. The end of the Albanian navy was very tragic. The good ship Herzegovina had been sent out as usual to bombard Kavaya; unfortunately she was brought in rather too close to the land and got stuck in a sandbank. The rebels, who had entrenched themselves on the seashore, opened fire and riddled all the deckhouses with bullets. The gunners were well protected by sand-bags, but the remainder of the ship's company had a most unpleasant quarter of an hour, before the ship was got off the sand and out of rifle range. The Austrian owners were apparently people of unwarlike disposition; anyway they objected to our using their ship as a man o' war, so the Albanian navy had perforce to disappear into the obscurity, whence it had come!

Chapter Twenty-Four

THE BEGINNING OF THE COLLAPSE

In the last chapter I gave a condensed account of the war news that kept reaching us daily during the last two months; the remainder of the story of the Albanian Kingdom; its gradual collapse and sudden ending, will occupy the rest of these pages.

In the early part of July we received the report of a speech made by Sir Edward Grey in the House of Commons, in the course of which he stated that Great Britain would on no account send any troops to Albania, but that there was no objection to any other of the powers doing so, if they thought fit to intervene on the Mbret's behalf. I had all along urged the King to appeal to Great Britain for help, as I thought that she at any rate, would remember that she had duties towards the child of her creation, so I was much astonished and pained at Sir Edward Grey's statement. No doubt the King was not a strong enough man to cope with the situation without the assistance of the European Concert. The Powers were quite justified in not having a very high opinion of him, but still he was doing his best and trying to keep his government clear of any undue foreign influence. This was no easy matter as the Austrians and Italians never ceased intriguing for power. The King was blamed for everything that went wrong and was made a scapegoat of by the Great Powers, who had unanimously promised their support. Now they refused to give it him; for instance the Epirus question was entirely beyond the King and ought to have been settled by the Concert of Europe. The powers behaved most discreditably, with the exception of Austria, who, if only for selfish reasons, would have been willing to help us, but was unable to do so, owing to the Italian jealousy.

During the early part of the month several small incidents took place at Durazzo, which though petty in themselves, were quite exciting at the time. So on the 5th of July it was reported that about 100 insurgents were crossing the swamps in open order; of course this news caused a stir in the palace and my brother, who was with me at the time, rushed off to his gun, on the hill behind the barracks. Imagine his surprise and disappointment, when the line of skirmishers turned out to be a flock of wild duck, having a morning's outing on the lagoon!

During that evening a Kosovan man went off his head, barricaded himself into a house behind the palace and threatened all passers-by with his rifle. A police officer came to us to inform us that it would probably be necessary to shoot the man. I urged him to do his best to avoid bloodshed and take the man alive, as there was always the danger of a blood-feud starting over a sudden death. Finally the lunatic was captured alive and shoved into the common gaol, there being no more suitable accommodation for him in the town, which never rose to the dizzy height of possessing a lunatic asylum of its own! On the following night, at about 10 o'clock, two shots were fired in the prison, not more than a hundred yards from my window, and the prisoners set up a great shout. I went out to see what had happened and met Baron Biegeleben, who had been installed practically as Chief of Police, and now arrived on the scene with a number of armed followers. Of course everybody, now always prepared for the worst, presumed that the prisoners had revolted. However it was soon discovered that the two shots had only been fired by the sentry on guard to call for help, as the mad Kosovan, who had been imprisoned on the previous night, had set fire to his bedding; this was easily put out and the remainder of the night passed peacefully.

On another occasion one of the gendarmes in the trenches had words with a Kosovan and shot him through the head, to enforce his argument; this again might have caused inter-tribal trouble! Luckily the gendarme too turned out to be a Kosovan, so the incident passed off without serious consequences; the murderer was not even arrested, but remained at his post. 24 hours later, just after 10 o'clock at night, he suddenly left his trench without any warning and, taking his rifle with him, disappeared in the darkness, making for the enemy's lines. His companions opened fire on him, to which he replied as soon as he reached cover and the result of it was that the fusillade soon became general on all sides and only ceased when messengers brought the news that the rebels had not been seen anywhere.

On the 7th of July a small Roumanian company of volunteers arrived at Durazzo; the men wore a self-invented but serviceable uniform, and were commanded by a Captain Cristescu of the Roumanian army. This Roumanian company was the first more or less disciplined body of men in the King's service and made a very good first impression. On the same ship were several Austrians, who had come out to take part in any fighting there might be; among these was Conte della Scala, an artillery officer, who made himself useful in organising the hill-positions, though he did not get any scrapping, as he had hoped to do. In spite of these reinforcements and the loyal messages received from all parts of the country, von Trotha and I clearly foresaw the end approaching rapidly; in this we were not alone, as the great majority of the foreign diplomats shared our views. Turkhan Pasha had been sent abroad to try to get help from one or other of the Powers; in the capitals of Europe, where he was known and esteemed as an honourable man and distinguished diplomat, he was well received. His reports to the King were very optimistic and the King and Queen still hoped that some good would come of his wanderings. Nothing that von Trotha or I said was taken seriously and when we spoke out our minds, which we did not infrequently, the Queen appeared to resent it; we received many a rebuff, but did not allow ourselves to be put off by anything and continued telling the King the unpleasant truths, which the other members of his Court kept hidden from him, as much as they were able. Persons most likely to know the truth told me time after time that the Powers were disappointed in him and would do nothing to help him, as they considered that he had proved himself unfit for his position. Though it may be considered bad form to tell one's employer all the uncomplimentary things that are said about him, I considered it a part of my duty to do so; perhaps it was taken amiss! Though the Queen disliked me, my regular correspondence with the King until the time of his death shows that, though he may not have appreciated my pessimism at the time, he fully realised that I had always done my best for him.

Everybody knew that our funds were running low, but I knew that which they did not, namely that the International Commission of Control would not help us in raising any more, when ours were finished. Of course I imparted my information to the King, but he could not believe its truth and kept on hoping that money would turn up from somewhere or other! There was nothing I could do to improve matters and it was frustrating to have to watch the Kingdom decaying before my eyes. In the town, where the people had bowed low at the very mention of the King's name, the unfortunate Mbret was now nicknamed "Burghermaster of Durazzo", and later even given the unflattering designation of "the Houseowner". One day one of the foreigners in the Albanian service alluded to him in this way in my presence, which much annoyed me, as he ought to have known better; he was a sensible fellow, he apologised for his want of tact.

As things were steadily going from bad to worse and I still believed that a few hundred Europeans would be sufficient to scatter the rebels, if properly led, I wrote to an Austrian sculptor, Mr. Gurschner,[51] who had on several occasions offered to bring out a certain number of volunteers. With the King's consent, I wrote to him privately, pointing out to him that we were in want of men; however I told him that all the men were likely to get in return for their services was lodging - in the trenches - and very coarse food. Gurschner, being a very energetic man, set to work with a will and besides appealing for volunteers in the Austrian press, opened a recruiting office in Vienna. The police of course had to sit up and take notice and the office had to be closed almost immediately. Large numbers of men had volunteered, but there was very little money available for their equipment and journey to Durazzo; a couple of small detachments reached us, not a hundred men in all, and the remainder were prevented from leaving Austria. Gurschner himself very nearly got into trouble with the Austrian authorities for trying to enlist men for a foreign power and as far as I remember he was, or just escaped, being arrested for this offence. About the middle of the month he appeared on the scene at Durazzo, where he remained for a few weeks. He got heartily sick of the place and returned to Vienna there to design an Albanian war medal; this however was never finished, as the Austro-Serbian war broke out and the artist had to join the army as a reserve officer.

One day the King, without the knowledge of his temporary Minister for Foreign Affairs, Mufid Bey Libohova, had a conference with the foreign ministers accredited to his Court on the Epirus question;[52] Mufid Bey took great offence at this quite unintentional slight and, being rather hot-tempered, sent in his resignation the same evening. Though Mufid was loyal to the throne and one of the most able ministers, he had a large number of enemies and we had received warnings that his life was in danger as long as he remained in office, so the King was not sorry at his decision to leave Durazzo a few days later. If I remember rightly he took up the post of Albanian Diplomatic Agent in Rome, which was vacant, owing to the disappearance of Dr Adamidi Bey Frasheri, who had been appointed some time earlier.

Several days after this rather unpleasant incident, a great meeting took place at the palace, presided over by the Mbret and attended by notables from all parts of the country.[53] The general situation was discussed and high-sounding speeches were made by some of those present; everybody expressed loyalty to the throne and hope for the future of Albania. However, nothing was done and things dragged on in the same slipshod way as before. About this time too Ahmed Bey Mati (Zog) issued a manifesto in the name of 150,000 Albanian Mahommedans; in this he pointed out that the rebels were only a very small minority in the country and that the bulk of the Mahommedans were loyal to the Mbret and willing to march to his support. He also mentioned that the rebellion was the work of foreign agitators and that no respectable Albanian should have anything to do with it. This cheered up the King and Queen, who still hoped to pull things through, or at least pretended to, though everybody else knew that their stay in Albania was absolutely bound to come to a conclusion in a short time.

Ahmed's manifesto was closely followed by a very curious counter-proclamation issued by the rebels, I believe, at Berat. After a certain amount of personal abuse directed against the King they called upon all patriotic Albanians to join them, as the insurrection had the support of the Triple Entente, and was bound to succeed in driving out the "foreign tyrant". Those in a position to judge said that the proclamation was well-worded and doubtlessly the work of a highly cultured person, probably a diplomat. This was the only time we heard anything about the Entente, though all along I felt that Italian influences were at work among the insurgents. That the neighbouring Balkan nations assisted them in every way, in order to keep Albania in a state of anarchy, seems extremely probable. However I do not pretend to be a politician, so I may be entirely wrong!

Chapter Twenty-Five

. . . .

THE END OF JULY

During the month of July a very close relationship sprang up between the King and Monsieur Ranette of the Roumanian legation. Ranette, though quite a young and very junior diplomat, used to come and see the King sometimes for hours on end, and sit with him in his study to discuss the situation with him.

Ranette was firmly convinced that everything could in time be settled peacefully, but how this was to be done, none of us were ever told; though he did not give one the impression that he was a man of action, he showed his self-confidence by going out to Kavaya and interviewing the insurgents, when these had refused to treat with the Mbret's government. As was to be expected, this intimacy caused a certain amount of jealousy and annoyance among some of the other diplomats, whose claim to get a hearing was much greater than that of Ranette, and there was a good deal of grumbling about it.

It seems certain that Monsieur Ranette did nothing really useful as far as the making of peace was concerned, but it was undoubtedly due to his work that Roumania began to take more interest in our affairs and sent us a certain number of soldiers and money. About the middle of the month, a second detachment of Roumanian volunteers arrived at Durazzo, so we now had almost a weak battalion of them at our disposal.

One thing Ranette succeeded in doing, which indirectly did the King's prestige a lot of harm, was to bring a certain Monsieur Kristo Mexi to the Court. Now Mexi was a banker, or retired banker, of Albanian origin, who had lived in Roumania for many years and had a very good position in that country. Unfortunately he was not so highly thought of in his own country and everybody was furious when the King appointed him as a Privy Councillor. The usual unproved charges were brought against him and a number of people went so far as to assure us that he had in his youth done time in Berat gaol for fraud. Von Trotha took an interest in this matter, but try as he could, no record of the imprisonment was to be found at Berat or any other town in Albania; so it must be presumed that there was no more truth in this story than there was in most of the others that one heard almost daily about some person or other. In spite of the abuse heaped upon him, Mexi held his ground and conferred with the King daily, and when I left Durazzo he was still coming to the palace regularly every morning. Probably we never noticed the insults that were heaped upon him, or regretted the fact that the Albanian members of the Court would have nothing to do with him and would not even shake hands with him! In their dislike for him they went so far that they would not even announce him to the King; so I usually had to do it for them, though it was not really my business.

On the 17th of July the King rode out to inspect the defences, accompanied by officers and some of the more notable volunteers. I was at first rather offended that he did not take me round with him on this occasion, as I was the only member of his suite who had taken any part in the fighting; besides which I was the only one who knew all our positions, none of the others ever having done the complete round of the trenches, as I did almost daily. As it turned out afterwards, I did not miss much by being left behind, as, when the King was inspecting the artillery position, there was quite a scene between some of the volunteers and the Dutch gendarmerie officers. The former delivered an uncalled-for criticism of the

Dutchmen's arrangements, which was naturally enough resented by the latter and altogether the King was placed in a very awkward position.

The next night there was a dinner party at the palace, at which, if I remember rightly, the three admirals were present. Anyway I distinctly recollect that Admiral Troubridge was one of our party. Some time after dinner, as the guests were about to take their departure, a heavy fusillade started all round the town; the party broke up quickly enough and I dashed to the Petroleum Magazine to see what the trouble was about. As I was wearing my full-dress tunic, which was rather tight, this night manoeuvre was not particularly pleasant and to make matters worse, I stepped onto a dried bog-hole in which I sank almost up to the armpits. It was a terrifying experience, but I managed to worm myself out under my own steam. This attack, as all the others, turned out to be nothing of any account; after firing a few volleys at us from a safe distance, the insurgents had retired, there being, of course, no losses on either side.

On the 18th July, the German Minister von Lucius told von Trotha that the King ought to retire gracefully before the powers, who had lost all faith in him, requested him to do so. As our old friendly relations with the King were disappearing, we found it rather hard to give him any unasked for advice; it was noticeable that both he and the Queen now only spoke to von Trotha and myself officially and hardly ever drew us into more private conversations. The Court was no longer the happy family it had been and our position was not a pleasant one. Naturally we were still expected to do all the work, as the Albanians were looked upon as ornaments only; however they got all the sweets!

The disorder in Durazzo was something awful, as the following example will show clearly enough. Twelve obsolete Austrian mountain guns, which were either a present from the Austrian government or sold to us for a purely nominal sum, arrived on the 20th, were partly unpacked and remained in the square with all the ammunition belonging to them for a couple of days; at the end of this time some person in authority took the trouble of having a look at them and discovered that all the breech-blocks were missing and the guns useless for the time being. Of course no serious steps were taken to find them, as it was far simpler to say that they had been stolen and thrown in the sea by the Italians, or that they had doubtlessly been left behind in Austria!

I had very little secretarial work to do at this time as the Mbret was far too busy to attend to his private affairs, so I got him to appoint me as a sort of Inspector-general of the forces, just to act as a check on the Dutch and other officers, some of whom were in a high state of inefficiency, whilst others spent their time quarrelling amongst themselves - not a useful occupation in a besieged town! My first duty was to try to find out what had happened to the lost breech-blocks. I spent the greater part of the afternoon riding round from one place to the other to make enquiries; at the custom-house they knew nothing about them, so I went on to the military store and, being unsuccessful here, to the police station. Nowhere had they been seen and I returned to the palace, my mission unfulfilled. A few minutes after my arrival, a telephone message came through from the stores that the missing blocks had been discovered there after all, the boxes in which they had arrived having been put away in the back of the shed with the harness by mistake.

As I was doing a round of the trenches that evening and was inspecting our picket at the bridge, heavy firing started in the town; thinking that the troops had mutinied, I galloped back for all I was worth, hoping to get through to the palace somehow. As I got near the town, I saw men shooting about the streets in a most disconcerting manner and must admit felt anything but happy. On coming up closer I discovered to my great relief that they were only firing into the air, or thereabouts; then I remembered that this was the eve of the feast of Ramadan and that the faithful welcome it with a feu de joie. As our noble warriors did not appear to be very particular as to where their shots would eventually lodge, I took my pony into a neighbouring cafe, in which we remained till the fusillade was over.

In the market square I found one of our foreign volunteers, an Austrian, surrounded by policemen, soldiers and townfolk, whom he was haranguing volubly; he was in a frantic state of excitement and kept yelling "Help - Murder - Revolution!" The crowd was doing its best to pacify him and trying to explain the national custom of shooting at the setting sun; however the worthy Austrian could not understand a word they said, and nearly fell round my neck when he saw me. I managed to satisfy him that there was no immediate danger and returned to the palace without any further incidents.

On the occasion of the feast of Ramadan, the insurgents sent a note to the foreign ministers, demanding the immediate removal of the Mbret, whom they described as a bloodthirsty tyrant, a lunatic and therefore quite unfit to govern. Failing this they threatened to level Durazzo to the ground and put its inhabitants to the sword; this note did not exactly add to the gaiety of the feast, but was not taken too seriously, though a certain number of agitators rushed round the town, as usual, spreading false rumours and scares.

Admiral Troubridge often came on shore in the evening and had a smoke with me in the garden; he quite realised how precarious was the King's position and foresaw that the Mbret would not be able to hold out much longer. His one hope was that he would retire in time and so avoid being driven out of his palace at a moment's notice. Like everybody else in the town, he could not understand why the Queen kept the two children in Durazzo during the summer as the town is notorious for its malarial fevers, and he would have been willing to give them a passage to Roumania or anywhere else on HMS Defence. During the next few days nothing of interest happened; the weather was very hot, but in spite of it, I spent half the day in the saddle, visiting the trenches, stores and hospitals. The rest of my time was taken up with my clerical and other duties, so I had as much work as one could wish for. Every night we sat up on the balcony enjoying the cool sea breezes, which were very refreshing after the stifling heat of the day. Unfortunately the evenings were usually disturbed by alarms and hardly a night passed without the rebels firing a volley or two at us before retiring to rest.

As there was no prospect of anything of real importance happening at Durazzo in the immediate future, the King decided to pay a visit to Valona, where the loyal Tosks were certain to give him a warm welcome.

Chapter Twenty-Six

. . . .

THE KING VISITS VALONA

At midnight on the 25th of July, the King, Queen and suite went on board the Misurata, which was to take us down to Valona; only von Trotha was left behind to look after the household and as a protection for the children, in case of any unforeseen trouble at Durazzo. As there were not enough cabins to go round, Ekrem Bey Libohova and I shared the small sitting room between us; as it was very stuffy in there, I remained on deck and went to sleep in a comfortable chair. I woke up at about two o'clock in the morning, as we were leaving the harbour and found that I was drenched to the skin, a very thick fog having come on while I was asleep. It was almost impenetrable and the ship's officers had to keep their wits about them in picking their way through the harbour, in which there were, besides the usual merchant craft, quite a number of men o' war of various descriptions. Our departure had not been made public as it was feared that it might be misconstrued and cause a panic; it was for this reason that we left in the dead of night when nobody was about to see us.

When we woke up next morning, we found ourselves close to land and soon after breakfast the Misurata entered Valona harbour. On our right lay the rocky island of Saseno, which protects the bay from the Easterly winds. The bay is sheltered on all sides; the hills come right down to the sea and in one place the hills might almost be termed mountains; they are grey and forbidding and remind one of the volcanic crags on the Asiatic side of the Red Sea, though here the lower slopes are cultivated. The harbour is large and safe and if it were in the interests of any power to do so, Valona could be turned into a second Hong-Kong and made practically impregnable from the sea side. The town of Valona, which lies some way back from the sea could also be defended quite easily from the land side, where there are rows of hills, forming natural ramparts to protect it.

The foreign sloops in the port fired a Royal salute, which awoke a thousand echoes among the hills and died away across the waters. Hardly had we dropped anchor, when the Governor, followed by one or two deputations, came out in his rowing boat; the oarsmen were wearing scarlet sweaters, which looked very bright in the morning sun and added gaiety to the scene. Among the deputations was one composed of Orthodox ladies; these being practically the first specimens of their kind and sex that I had seen in Albania, where most of the upper classes hide their womenfolk, we naturally took more interest in them than in the frock-coated dignitaries of the town.

By the landing-stage huge crowds of enthusiastic Tosks were assembled and here too the Commandant of the town and other officials welcomed the sovereigns. The American volunteer, Mr. Spencer, whom the King had commissioned to furnish a guard of honour for this occasion, had drawn up his men, consisting to a great extent of war-worn veterans, on three sides of the square. The King inspected them and expressed his satisfaction at their smart appearance. They were not as picturesque as our northern mountaineers, having discarded the national Fustanella[54] for a more serviceable khaki uniform, but they appeared to be more disciplined and it is certain were on the whole more highly educated (Many of them could read and write!). We were all surprised to find the late Court doctor attached to this guard of honour; with his imposing tropical helmet and Mauser rifle slung across his shoulder, he looked a very bold warrior, but in spite of his martial aspect and pretended importance, he was quietly ignored by everybody.

The inspection over, the King and Queen got into a carriage which had been raised from God knows where to take them into the town. The crowd unharnessed the horses and men took their place, dragging the carriage along the dusty road, which crosses the marshy plain. The King and Queen were all right, but the unhappy suite was not so well cared for and was left standing disconsolately in the market square. As a matter of fact we were nearly trampled under foot by the enthusiastic mob and did not appreciate the idea of a two mile walk, which seemed the only alternative to remaining here at the harbour the rest of the day. At last a two-horse vehicle, occupied by four or five well nourished notables approached us; Ekrem Bey stopped it, made the occupants get out and commandeered it for ourselves; it was about the most ramshackle old thing I ever saw and the half starved nags could hardly drag it. Our progress was slow, but this did not disturb us, as it gave us all the more time to study our surroundings.

The port is separated from the town by a stretch of low lying, park-like land, which was dried up by the sun and grey with dust, though it is a swamp during the winter months. Over the grass the crowds followed us on foot, on horseback, any way they could, jumping small ditches on the way, or falling into them, to the great delight of their neighbours. The funniest sight of the lot were two well-fed and elderly citizens of Valona, who were sharing a poor little twelve-hand pony, which was continually making frantic efforts to rid itself of the double burden. The dust was something awful, but did not check the enthusiasm of the Valonese, who seemed to have gone off their heads with joy.

This enthusiasm was, I verily believe, perfectly genuine, as the Tosks understand what patriotism means, in its larger sense, while the northern mountaineers are more loyal to their clan chieftains than to their country, and too ignorant to have any very high political ideals. It must also be remembered that Albanian independence was first proclaimed here at Valona by Ismail Kemal Vlora,[55] so it is only natural that the Valonese, who considered themselves the founders of the Kingdom, gave their Mbret such an enthusiastic reception.

At last, smothered in dust, we arrived at the Vloras' family mansion, where the King established his headquarters for the day. We were received at the door by Ekrem Bey Vlora, who is already known to the reader, and other members of his family. The house itself is large and roomy, rather larger than the Palace at Durazzo and it would certainly have made a better Royal residence, if a little money had been spent on it. Owing to the anarchy prevailing in Albania, Ekrem's father, who was now Albanian minister in Vienna, had thought it advisable to remove most of the valuables from the house, so there was very little furniture left in it now and in fact only one wing could be used for the reception. There was nothing worth mentioning about the house; there were few pictures on the walls and the only one I noticed was a large oil painting, representing Ferid Pasha, the owner's brother, who was for a time Grand Vizier in Constantinople and now lived a retired life in Egypt.[56]

A certain number of people were assembled to be presented to the sovereigns and, as soon as we had made ourselves halfway presentable, deputations began to arrive. Then followed the usual dull ceremonial, which was so boring that it is not worth describing. The only point worth mentioning about these deputations is, that the spokesmen were unanimous in emphasising the atrocities of the Greek and Epirote bands, which had devastated the Northern Epirus. A deputation of Bektashi Mahommedan monks[57] told the King how the Greeks had burned their monastery and laid waste the surrounding country; it was touching to see these venerable old men appealing to their young Mbret for advice and assistance. They showed such childlike confidence that he would be able to put matters right, not only for them, but for the whole country! Here in Valona one really had the feeling that the Albanians were not all brigands, as they are supposed to be, but thinking men with national ideals and political aspirations! After the most horrible tales of woe, some of which were probably based on fact, the leader of a deputation would smile and murmur "Rroft Mbreti", which was fervently seconded by his followers, as if the King's welfare were all that really mattered.

A number of Albanian gendarmerie officers were presented to the King, who spoke to the few who had distinguished themselves in the fighting against the Epirotes and the central Albanian insurgents. With these was Captain Ghilardi, who had done such good work all along. After an endless series of deputations had been received in audience and sent away with words of encouragement, the company assembled for dinner. This was a European meal, served as well as can be expected under the circumstances; our hosts, however did not take part, but waited on their guests in person, having their dinner, when everybody else had finished. From the time of our arrival, large crowds had collected outside the gates and kept cheering, to which the King and Queen had to respond by appearing on the balcony again and again, to thank them for the ovation. As this was a busy day, we were not given much time for coffee and cigarettes after the meal and soon had to set out again, to have a look at the town and its immediate surroundings, as well as to allow the loyal people of Valona to make their sovereigns' closer acquaintance.

Chapter Twenty-Seven

. . . .

VALONA

In the last chapter I omitted to mention the following rather unpleasant incident, which took place during the morning. When the gendarmerie officers arrived to be presented to the King, they were accompanied by Ghilardi and Spencer, which was only natural and proper, as these two had acted as officers for months past and had seen a lot of fighting in the Epirus, besides which, Spencer had been ordered to raise a bodyguard for the King's visit to Valona. Major Sluys, more or less commandant of the town, for some reason unknown to us, did not allow Spencer to enter the house; it was known that the two were not the best of friends, as Spencer had criticised in rather strong language the conduct of the Dutch officers, who are said to have left him in the lurch during the retirement from Koritza.

In spite of Major Sluys' objections, Spencer managed to slip through the police cordon and into the house; he got as far as the waiting room on the first floor, from where he sent a messenger to fetch me. I found him in a great state of excitement and indignant at the manner in which he had been treated. While I was with him, two gendarmes appeared in the room to arrest him. I ordered them to stand back and await further instructions from me and approached the King to ask him what I was to do; the latter, without hesitation, ordered

Spencer to be admitted. When I returned to the waiting room, I found it empty, but heard a "fracas" going on downstairs. It appeared that as soon as I had left Spencer, Major Sluys had arrested him, in spite of my interference. Spencer had resisted arrest and in the course of the struggle had been thrown, or bustled down the stairs in a very rough manner by his captors. Now I found them assembled in the hall, surrounded by a host of serving men and soldiers, who had run together to watch the sport. I told the Major to release his prisoner instantly; I was furious at his high-handed action and asked him whether this was his idea of treating an officer, also pointing out to him that Spencer was an American and anyway not under his jurisdiction. Sluys, though he remained cool outwardly, was very truculent and most unwilling to give up his captive. He informed not only me, but the public at large, of the fact that Spencer was not only not an officer, but the biggest liar, boaster and coward in the country and had done nothing but flee before the enemy on every occasion that they appeared. As I knew that this was not true and had Ghilardi on the spot to disprove this, and in fact knew that Spencer had done very useful work, I entirely lost it and told Major Sluys one or two home truths that cannot have pleased him to any great extent. I advised him not to insult any of the foreign volunteers, as some of them had behaved far more creditably than one or two of the Dutch officers, who were drawing high salaries for their services, while they were drawing none. As a parting shot I mentioned that I was going to write a report on the Dutch gendarmerie mission, which would contain some unfavourable criticism on some of its officers. This last was not at all to the Major's liking, and no wonder! The Dutch officers were receiving enormous salaries while serving in Albania, and some of them at least did not want to lose the remunerative little billets they held there. It was an unfortunate occurrence, this difference of opinion, and unfortunately did not end here, but caused further unpleasantness later on.

The victory for the moment was mine and the onlookers were delighted that I had gained my point; more especially as

Major Sluys appears to have succeeded in making himself disliked by the Valonese, though he had been one of the most popular men in Albania when he had taken up his post there. In fact, at that time, owing to the important part he had played in the Essad "coup", he had been looked upon as one of the liberators of Albania. However, now his position was decidedly weak; owing to differences with the civil authorities, he had resigned his post some days earlier and an Albanian commandant had been appointed in his place. As soon as the King's visit to the town was announced, he had changed his mind and reappointed himself as commandant. Rather a curious state of affairs in a country not six hours from European civilisation! Owing to the mystery still surrounding all these transactions, the Major was not invited to the King's luncheon and, as all the other notables were present, this must have been rather galling to him; altogether it was not a pleasant day for him!

Well, to go on with the story! After lunch we went out to have a look at the town and to impress the population. The King, Ekrem, Selim and I were mounted by our host and a carriage was provided for the Queen and the two ladies in waiting. Our escort consisted of half a dozen fine looking Southern chiefs, wearing the national costume and a detachment of Spencer's khaki-clad Tosks. As we rode through the town, we were soon surrounded by an enthusiastic crowd, which accompanied us through the streets. As our progress threatened to be brought to standstill altogether by so much loyalty we put the horses to a trot and so escaped, though a certain number of the younger men were not to be shaken off so easily and ran along beside the horses through the gaily decorated streets and out into the country! On the hills behind the town thousands of refugees from the ravaged districts were encamped and the woods seemed to be teeming with them. Men, women and children came rushing down to us from all sides to get a better view of the King and, in spite of the fact that these unfortunates had lost everything they possessed, they showed no less enthusiasm than their more fortunate brothers of the town. The road was shockingly bad and the Queen's drive cannot have been much of a pleasure, particularly as the horses continually jibbed and had to be dragged along bodily by the crowd - quite a picture it was!

On our return to the "Palais Vlora", we were given fruit syrups and crushed ice, a national drink in southern Albania, which was excellent and much relished by us, as we were again half choked with the dust. As there was no work to be done for the present, I was taken to the Haremlik, to visit the ladies of the family, who had so far not appeared on the scene, according to the best traditions of the Mahommedan world. This visit has nothing sensational about it; the ladies, all of whom were well-educated and able to speak several languages, which is a good deal more than is often the case in England, received me, just the same as any European ladies would have done and there was nothing whatsoever to remind one of imagines as a harem, except in the name. After all the native dignitaries, with the exception of a few members of the Vlora family, had left, the ladies came over to the other part of the house, to be presented to the King, and they remained with us until we left.

In Albania the ladies are kept secluded, as in Turkey, but this appears to be done chiefly for show, to keep up appearances, and they do not seem to be particular when foreigners are concerned and do not mind being seen by them. For instance the Aide de Camp's wife stayed in the palace, as the Queen's guest, for several months and was never veiled in the house; she was quite one of us, as long as no other Mohammedans were about. However she was not even allowed to go into the garden without a veil, and when we gave a dinner at which Albanians were present, she did not appear till they had gone. In the mountains the women go about unveiled, like the Arab women, who are very strict Mahommedans all the same. The veiling was, I believe, a purely Turkish national custom or fashion which gradually spread to the whole Mahommedan world.

After tea we left the town of Valona amidst a cheering populace. Close to the quay the King and Queen inspected the hospital of the Dutch gendarmerie mission, which was well-situated, close to the sea and in perfect order; the Dutch surgeon in charge of it did splendid work in it and his patients were full of praise for him.

From here we went back to our faithful Misurata; we left the harbour at about 5 o'clock, witnessing a most glorious sunset, which was followed by an oriental starlit night. After dinner we stayed on deck, little groups of two and three were formed and, at peace with the world, we rested from our labours. That night we were again very optimistic, as the enthusiasm of the Tosks had made a great impression on us; we hoped that after all we might succeed in doing the impossible with the help of the loyal southerners!

Sailing close to the coast all the time, we saw the fires of the rebels, camped on the shore, close to the mouth of the Skumbi river, and, after a very pleasant voyage, arrived at Durazzo in the early hours of the morning. Everybody was tired, so the party soon broke up, everybody feeling a good deal more hopeful after all we had seen and heard at Valona. Unfortunately, things are not always what they seem; Valona did not help us as we had hoped and only a few months afterwards was occupied by the Italians, who will not give it up again now that they have their hands on it. It is invaluable to them, as in conjunction with Otranto, it turns the Adriatic into an 'Italian Lake', thus preventing the Austrians from becoming a Mediterranean Power.

Chapter Twenty-Eight

. . . .

THE LAST MONTH

The King's visit to Valona was the last interesting event that took place, while I was in Albania and the rest of my experiences can be told in a few words. Our life remained much as it had been during the last six weeks and I had plenty of work to keep me busy, though my functions as private secretary did not bother me much, the King being far too harassed to be able to attend to his private affairs.

The greater part of my day I spent making tours of inspection, often doing two rounds of the positions during the day, to see that everything was in order. At this time we had a lot of sickness among the men and there were hundreds of cases of malaria, dysentery and other ailments in the trenches. The native doctors, who spent their time trying to find soft government billets, were far too lazy to attend to them, so I made it my business to make them do so, like or no like! I used to commandeer a doctor and take him round the positions; some of the Roumanian volunteers had to accompany us with stretchers and medicines and so I saw that something was done for our men, who would otherwise have been left unattended where they were. The Queen organised an Albanian hospital, where there was room for a certain number of patients, but not enough for them all, so a good many of them had to be lodged in private houses in the town.

As secretary of the Order of the Eagle of Albania, I also had a certain amount of work, as lists had to be prepared for the King, who decorated people almost daily, usually with the lowest class, a bronze medal "for gallantry in the field". As it was found to be quite impossible to decorate only the deserving soldiers without offending all the rest, the plan was adopted of decorating all the wounded, irrespective of merit, and this worked fairly well. The Albanians loved their medals and even wore them on their nightshirts; it is a pity that the King did not bring a larger supply of them, as I believe that he could have increased his popularity enormously by distributing them more freely.

There was rather an echo of the Valona incident between Major Sluys and myself; though it sounds ridiculous enough now, it was most unpleasant at the time. One morning General de Veer came for an audience with the King, as he often did, and, as usual, was shown into the waiting room, next to my office, where Sami Bey entertained the more notable visitors. Hearing that he had arrived, I went over to him with the intention of reporting Major Sluys' strange conduct in regard to Spencer. The General did not get up, when I entered the room, and refused to shake hands with me, when I went up to him. I was more than surprised at his rudeness, as we had always been on excellent terms with each other, and felt much annoyed, as Sami Bey was present to witness the insult. I asked the General the reason for his behaviour and he spluttered out some reply, which I failed to catch. As he was bubbling over with indignation and could not be brought to reason, I left him, with a few well-chosen words, which exactly expressed my feelings, but were perhaps not quite as parliamentary as one would expect to hear in the King's waiting room. Later I discovered that the General was so angry, because I had told Sluys that I was going to write a report on the Dutch gendarmerie mission; as he himself was thoroughly inefficient, this is not really surprising. Nobody in Durazzo could have said much good about him as a soldier, or bad as a man.

Mr. Lamb of the Commission of Control tried to pacify him

for me, but he was quite childish in his wrath and refused to apologise for his rudeness. It was a most unpleasant situation for me, as his age prevented me from taking sterner measures and an "affair of honour" was to be avoided under all circumstances for the King's sake. So we remained au froid and, though having to come in contact with each other very frequently, did not know each other for the rest of the time.

The news of the murder of the Austrian Archduke Franz Ferdinand on 28 June 1914 made a deep impression on the Court, but none of us thought that it would ever bring on anything more than strained relations between Austria and Serbia. Some thought that it would simplify the accession difficulty in the dual monarchy, which was bound to arise on the death of the aged Emperor. The Archduke Francis Ferdinand was not universally popular in the Austro-Hungarian Empire and it was only the manner of his death that brought him the sympathies of the people.

When we heard that Russia and Germany had started mobilising, von Trotha was delighted, as in this he saw a chance of retiring gracefully from the Court of Albania, without giving offence to the King and Queen. On the 1st of August he left us, though the German Minister von Lucius had not received any official information about a general mobilisation; he was accompanied by his secretary and five other menservants, who were German army reservists. Their sudden departure made a big hole in our establishment and we were now left with only three indoor men-servants, the English butler, the King's old German valet, who only belonged to the Landsturm and the Queen's Arab servant, Hassan. Sami Bey, who ought really to have succeeded Trotha by right of seniority, was not keen on work and understood little or nothing about book-keeping, so I undertook the difficult task of running, or trying to run the shrunken household. My first duty was to pacify the women servants, who came to me en bloc to give notice; the majority of them wanted to leave by the next boat, as "they were afraid of staying on, now that the men had gone", and it was as much as I could do to "blarney" them into staying with us for the time being at least. I believe that they had a second attack of nerves not long afterwards, but the Queen pacified them on that occasion.

During the last days of July signs were not wanting that war was in the air; the most notable was the manner in which the international fleet melted away. First the small Russian cruiser Askold left in the dead of night, without giving any notice to anybody; nobody knew where she had gone, but the commander of the French cruiser "presumed" that she had gone to Brindisi to coal. The French left us in the same mysterious manner a couple of nights later and was in due course followed by HMS Defence, which had to leave one evening at short notice. The Breslau and Austrian ships left a few days after this and our friends, the Italians remained as our sole protectors, the ancient Dandolo taking the place of a more modern vessel. They saw the end approaching rapidly and did not bother the King in any way, or take any advantage of their supreme position in Durazzo to further their own ends. They knew that Valona, like a ripe plum, would drop into their hands when the time came, so they could afford to be generous and wait.

Another curious thing that happened in the second half of July, which now seems rather suggestive. Having heard from an absolutely reliable source that Messrs. Ehrhardt, the second largest gun manufacturers in Germany, had a few guns of medium bore in stock, the Albanian government made enquiries through an agent, as it was thought that with a 10 or 15 cm. gun we would be able to bombard the insurgents' headquarters at Shjak and perhaps even at Kavaya from the hill behind Durazzo. Messrs Ehrhardt now informed us that they were sorry to say they had no unsold guns of medium bore in their factories. Of course, our original informant may have been mistaken, but it does not seem probable, as he was in a position to know. It is more likely that the German government had already warned the larger manufacturers not to allow any more munitions of war to leave the country.

One evening we had a tremendous scene in the palace; Turkhan Pasha, who, after his tour round Europe, had a very black and faithful servant, whom he had bought as a boy in Constantinople, over twenty years ago. One day Turkhan wanted to dress for dinner and was unable to do so, as his servant was missing; the old gentleman was very anxious about him and afraid that he had met with some accident. After making enquiries all over the place, it was at length discovered that he had been arrested for some treason and lodged in gaol! When Turkhan heard of his unhappy valet's fate, he nearly had a fit. He sent for the Chief of Police and his protests being of no avail, he went to the King and threatened him with his immediate resignation failing his man's release.

The only evidence against him seemed to be that he had been seen about in the company of a suspicious character, and that he had waved his white handkerchief during a walk on the hill behind the barracks, close to the chief gun-position. Some people even asserted that he had signalled messages over to the insurgents. As a matter of fact the poor black had never served in the army and so it is most unlikely that he knew anything about signalling, besides which it was found that he could neither read nor write; so it is evident that he was the victim of a mistake or an intrigue. Anyway the King had him released and restored to his master, who was dreadfully upset by the incident, which he believed was a put up job to discredit him in the eyes of the King. Turkhan's loyalty to the throne was always questioned by some of the ultra-nationalists and it is possible that they decided to get hold of the man and get incriminating evidence against his master through him.

We began to have quite a lot of trouble with the garrison, which cannot be wondered at, when one remembers that it consisted mainly of irregulars. Many of the Mirdites kept leaving us in small detachments, and not a few sold the rifles that had been served out to them on their arrival in Durazzo. One could buy rifles of the most modern patterns from five to ten francs a piece! On the 2nd of August a few Malissori had a little dispute in the main street, in the course of which, as was at that time customary in the Balkans, one or two shots were exchanged; terrible rumours were immediately put into circulation by interested parties and the usual panic followed, as the population was becoming so hysterical that it believed every ridiculous yarn that was told them.

On the same day Mr. Lamb and General de Veer went over to Shjak to negotiate with the insurgents for the release of the two Dutch officers, who had fallen into their hands at Elbasan, but as far as I can recollect they were not successful. In the evening most of the Austrian and German volunteers, who had formed the backbone of our resistance, left Durazzo, to join their respective armies. They were most enthusiastic and made a great demonstration outside the palace, cheering and singing German patriotic songs. On landing in Italy they tried the same sort of thing, but the police at the port of Bari had to protect them from the crowd, who did not appreciate their allies' warlike sentiments. The King decorated all the foreign volunteers, as well they deserved; bronze medals were not expensive and gave great pleasure. The officers were given the fourth and fifth classes of the order, according to their rank, and those that had particularly distinguished themselves in the field got small crossed swords attached to their decorations.

Two days later the officers of the Dutch gendarmerie mission were recalled by their government and left with a certain number of volunteers, who, not belonging to the first reserve, had remained behind to await developments.

When there were rumours of war in the air and I found myself as the only person left to do the work; I told the King that I would be willing to remain with him, if I could get leave off any mobilisation in England, as I did not want to leave him in the lurch at the very last. I did not believe in the possibility of war and thought that, even if one should break out, there would still be plenty of time for me to rejoin my regiment after the break-up of Albania, which I knew could not be delayed many weeks. So the King telegraphed to Sir Edward Grey, through Mr. Lamb, and I was ordered to remain at my post until further notice.

Our war news was contradictory in the extreme, as we had to rely mainly on Austrian official telegrams and Italian local papers, all of which were very unreliable. We read of bloody engagements which never took place and of victories that were never won. It was a bad time for us altogether; as the Austrian Lloyd had suspended its service to Durazzo, we were no longer able to get our regular supplies from Trieste and had perforce to buy rather inferior goods in the South of Italy. Our head chef, though a German reservist, was luckily not by nature a great warrior, so was quite agreeable to staying on with us on the strength of a doctor's certificate which I obtained for him that he was not fit for service.

The state of the country was becoming more and more chaotic and I repeatedly advised the King to give up his thorny throne. As things were absolutely hopeless, I also proposed to the King that we should at least drink up the good wines we had in the cellar and leave the inferior sorts for our successors. Unfortunately this brilliant idea was treated with scorn and so it came to pass that many of the King's most excellent hocks remained un-drunk.

Every night the insurgents fired volleys, just to keep us awake, and occasionally honoured us with a feeble night attack, which always ended in noise and smoke, without hurting anybody on either side. On one occasion, by way of a change, they fired two shots at us with one of the guns they had captured, but failed to hit the town, which it must be supposed was what they were aiming at.

After the departure of the Dutch officers a Committee of Defence was formed, consisting of a few Austrians who had not yet been called to the colours, a Roumanian officer and two or three native chieftains. They worked very hard to strengthen our position, though we were becoming weaker every day, owing to the desertion of the tribesmen; these were suffering considerably from the heat and the unsanitary conditions in the trenches and, considering that they had served quite long enough for the time being, made everything an excuse to return to their homes.

On the 13th of August the Albanian Government had no cash left and I was ordered to supply the money for paying the troops out of the Court funds. I did this with a very bad grace, as I knew that what we had left was barely enough for our own requirements. Owing to this and other difficulties which had arisen, I handed the keys of the safe over the King a couple of days later.

Everybody urged the King to leave, while there was still time, but he would not listen to anybody, not even to the German Minister, who certainly took an interest in his welfare. He would not understand that he was played out and that his own men would turn on him as soon as his money came to an end; but of course he still hoped in a vague sort of way that money would be forthcoming from somewhere! How he could believe such a thing surpasses my understanding, considering that he knew the Italian standpoint well enough and it was not likely that Austria, a chronically impecunious country in times of peace, could possibly afford to send him gold at such a time. The King must have been about the most optimistically inclined person in the world, or have had more reserve energy than one would have been led to suspect. He was absolutely alone in his optimism and one must give him the credit that is due to him for holding out for weeks and months after everybody had advised him to give it up as a bad job and leave!

Chapter Twenty-Nine

GOODBYE TO DURAZZO

For some time past I had been becoming dissatisfied with the manner in which I was being treated. Already before the outbreak of war, the King and Queen had been noticeably cool in their conduct towards von Trotha and myself. When Trotha left Durazzo on the 1st of August I missed him very much, as we had been on excellent terms with each other all the time and I now found myself left with nobody to discuss things with. Selim Bey, who was a very cheery boy, had been sent north on some errand and was absent till the day I left. Ekrem Bey and I, though we were always on good terms, very rarely exchanged confidences. Sami Bey used to retire to his own house as soon as he had finished his duties, and I therefore did not see so much of him. The royal coolness towards myself became so marked that everybody at Court noticed it and talked about it. The climax of this tension was reached one night at dinner when the Queen, in the course of a political lecture on the European War, in which I had taken no part, said: "Everybody knows that the English soldiers are quite bad". I nearly choked with indignation, but said nothing, and the King tried to change the subject, looking most uncomfortable. Afterwards, when I got him his after-dinner cigar, I asked him whether I was to take the Queen's remark as a hint that I was no longer wanted and assured him that I would be ready to leave by the next boat, if that were the case. He was very apologetic and said it was all a mistake, or words to that effect, so, honour being satisfied, I let the matter drop. On this occasion the King once again behaved very well, seeing that I was quite in the right.

What was the cause of the coolness, I cannot imagine and nobody else could think of any possible explanation. Perhaps I had been too outspoken or it is possible that somebody had intrigued against me, not an unheard of occurrence at Court. Surely the following unfortunate incident cannot have been the cause of it all! One day we were sitting together in the Oriental Room and happened to discuss the Queen's "regal" manner of treating people; in the course of the conversation I remarked that she had no more reason to be haughty than I had, as the only reason that my border-raiding ancestors had not annexed her family's petty principality, was the fact that there was not enough booty to be found in it. At this point somebody looked round the corner of the passage and discovered that the Queen was sitting there with her work-basket. Perhaps she heard our conversation and disapproved of the tone; certainly it was an unfortunate occurrence, which, with a little more care, might have been avoided!

Practically nothing now remains to be told but what led to my retirement from the arena. It had been arranged that the children were to be sent to Germany, as at last it was realised how precarious our position at Durazzo had become; they were originally to have been accompanied by Fräulein von Oidtmann. On the 20th of August Fräulein von Pfuel informed me just before dinner that she had been told to pack her belongings and leave with the children on the 22nd of August, as the position was so uncertain that women would only be in the way. At the same time the Queen told her that I was going to be dismissed too, though she did not give any reason for this. I was very pleased that at last my advice was being followed and that both ladies were being sent away out of danger; for months past I had considered that Durazzo was no place for them, as one could hardly go half a mile outside the town without the risk of being shot at. However I was much surprised to hear that

I too was going to be got rid of, and very angry that this should
be discussed publicly before I had been told about it.

I waited for the King to say something to me on the subject
after dinner, but as he did not make any attempt to do so before
retiring into his study, I followed him and asked him straight
out whether it was true that he intended dismissing me. He was
anything but at his ease and at first would not give me a clear
answer. However, at last he said that he was thinking of
dismissing me, as things could not go on here in this way, and
he was certain that I wanted to go to the front and that I held
different political opinions to his. In fact he seemed hard-
pressed to find some reasonable pretext, but could not invent
one on the spur of the moment. I had expressed my willingness
to remain with him to the end and had got leave to do so only
three weeks earlier; secondly I had rarely, if ever, expressed any
opinions on the European War, except to him privately, always
having avoided political conversations for fear of giving
offence. One evening, it is true, when left alone with the King
on the balcony, I told him that I thought that the German
government had gone mad. I may also have pointed out to him
that Germany had lost the war on the day that Great Britain
had joined in, but I believe that he did not think much
differently himself, as he had a very real idea of her power! As
has already been mentioned, I was fed-up with the way I had
been treated recently and this sudden dismissal seemed to be
the last straw!

I tried not to show the irritation that I felt and only
remarked that I was exceedingly sorry if I had given offence to
anybody, as I had all along done my best to further the King's
interests and had worked myself to death for him. He answered
in a half-hearted sort of way, that he had been quite satisfied
with me, but that all the same it was better for me to leave.

The King was speaking generally and I do not believe really
wished me to leave at once, but I was annoyed by his seeming
ingratitude and expressed my intention of leaving on the same
day as the royal children. Since I left Durazzo and had the
opportunity of reading of certain developments there after my

departure, I have begun to think that the King may have had the following motive for dismissing me.

Although the Albanian government had declared its neutrality in the European conflict, bands were being formed against the Serbians before I left Durazzo. The government knew of this and did not attempt to put a stop to the movement; in fact it secretly supported it and one of the ex-ministers, Hasan Bey Prishtina, became one of its leaders. I believe that the King was not in favour of this policy, but was not strong enough to put his foot down and arrest the leaders. Perhaps he decided to get rid of me, as I might have reported any further warlike preparations to the British Government.

After resigning, I left the King thoroughly huffed and retired to the Oriental room to sulk with the others. By and by I regained my temper and remembered some of the many kindnesses done to me by the King; for instance, how it had never been thrown in my face that I had lost the 40,000 francs of Court money on the 23rd of May and how the King had immediately made good my personal loss on that occasion. On thinking things over, I decided that there was nothing to prevent me from escorting the children to Germany and so rendering the King a last parting service. I went back to the study and proposed this to him; he jumped at the idea, as travelling on the continent might have been none too pleasant for the ladies alone. He was however uncertain about my being able to procure the necessary safe-conducts.

Next morning I went to see the German minister, with whom I was on excellent terms in spite of the war, and he told me that there would be no difficulty in giving me a safe-conduct, which would see me safely in and out of Germany. The Austro-Hungarian minister also telegraphed to his government to allow me to pass through the Tyrol there and back and, on receiving a favourable reply, he too was able to furnish me with the necessary document. During the day I did my last round of the trenches and said goodbye to my friends, who were much surprised at my sudden departure; the rest of my time I had to spend packing, as the German valet had been replaced by an

Albanian, who had once been a bottle washer in some hotel in America and knew nothing about clothes, packing, or anything else connected with a valet's various duties.

Before we left on the 22nd, the King called me into his study and presented me with the Order of the Eagle of Albania (with crossed swords), the Accession medal and a signed photograph of himself, on which he had written "In remembrance of joint labours". He could not possibly have been more charming than he was and thanked me warmly for all I had done to help him, adding that he would welcome me back, should things take a turn for the better.

In fact I felt so softened towards him, that I thought of putting my pride in my pocket and remaining at Durazzo till the King himself was forced to flee; that this was bound to happen in the course of a few weeks I felt absolutely certain. He also gave me an excellent testimonial, in which he gave the European War as the cause for my leaving his service, so we parted the best of friends, which makes his subsequent conduct towards me all the more inexplicable. On this last day, too, the Queen was again quite friendly towards me (the ladies in waiting thought it was because I was leaving).

The Italian minister had all arrangements made for our journey as far as the Austrian frontier and also gave me a letter of recommendation to the Italian Minister in Munich. To everybody's surprise, we found that Captain Conte Andreoli of the Italian legation, was going to escort us as far as Ala, the Austrian frontier station. The King was very liberal in my travelling expenses, so with plenty of cash and the Austrian and German safe-conducts in my pocket, I looked forward to a pleasant and instructive journey. Unfortunately, I did not take a certain diplomat's warning when he told me that I could trust a Kaffir's safe-conduct, or even an Austrian, but that the German Government did not understand the meaning of the word "honour" and would probably break its pledge towards me! I thought that I knew the Germans better than he did and had confidence in them.

After tea we left Durazzo, the two royal children, two

nurses, the ladies in waiting, the chef, whose conscience was beginning to prick him, and I. On the Italian ship, which was to convey us to Bari, we were met by Conte Andreoli. Looking across at the palace, we saw the King and Queen on the balcony waving to us and we felt sorry for them; they had hoped for so much and, in spite of continual work and worry, had attained nothing! We had had an interesting time here, in this dusty sun-baked Durazzo, with its white-washed hovels and dark, ragged gipsies! I had dreamed of remaining here and making a career and now it was rapidly disappearing in the dusk. The three lonesome poplars by the seashore, our favourite evening walk, we saw for the last time and then they too vanished in the gloom! We were all of us very depressed and occupied with our own thoughts, so it was not a cheerful meal we sat down to that night by any means. "Partir c'est mourir un peu.": that is what we all thought on closing this most interesting chapter in our lives. So it came to pass that I disappeared again into obscurity, whence it had pleased the Mbret to call me for a few brief months.

Epilogue

. . . .

HUMPTY DUMPTY HAD A GREAT FALL

In the foregoing pages I have tried to give an account of my experiences in Albania, so the book ought really to end with my departure from Durazzo. However I am adding this short epilogue, as the reader may be interested to hear how disastrously the whole adventure ended for all parties concerned in it.

As I was the first to suffer, I will tell in a few lines what fate had in store for me. Our journey through Italy and the Tyrol may be skipped, and only mention be made of the fact that we arrived in Munich late on the 26th of August, and that the children continued their journey to Waldenburg on the morning of the 28th. My mission being now accomplished, I decided to leave for Bari, where I had left my luggage, next morning, intending to return to England from Italy. I had been exceedingly courteously treated by the Austrian and also by the Bavarian authorities. Complying with the regulations then in force for foreigners, I reported myself to the police. A second safe-conduct, ratifying the original one, was procured for me by the Italian minister from the Bavarian foreign office and was countersigned by the military authorities; so I thought that I was absolutely safe and that no difficulties would be put in my way. However I was soon undeceived. The police did not know what to make of me and sent me on to the military headquarters with a plain-clothes detective. At the "Generalkommando", the officer in charge examined my papers and seemed quite satisfied. I was on the point of leaving his office a free man, when he said that I was at liberty to travel, if I could state as an officer and gentleman that I really intended to return to my duties at Durazzo. Having already left the King's service, I was of course unable to give my word that I would do so and could only protest against any new stipulations being made. However protest was useless and I had to give parole not to leave Munich for the present. I was otherwise absolutely free and able to communicate with the King; I informed him of my predicament telegraphically and asked him to recall me, as I would then be allowed to go. I followed this up with a letter, in which I wrote him the full facts of the case and pointed out to him, that I would be able to leave on receipt of a wire from him. The days passed and I wrote one letter after the other asking for help; but no reply came, though I know for a fact that some, if not all, of my communications reached their destination.

When I spent a day with the King - now the ex-King - in Vienna in 1937, he explained to me that my recall had been made quite impossible by the German legation, who had been urging him to get rid of me as soon as the war started, as it was thought that I could raise the northern clans, among whom the devoted work of Miss Edith Durham had done much to create a pro-British feeling, which might have counter-acted their hatred for the Serbians. The German authorities could not understand the King's silence and more than one German officer expressed his condemnation of the manner in which I had been treated, not only by the German government, but also by the King, when a line from him would have saved me. The Germans did not molest me, but in spite of their expressions of sympathy, I woke up one morning to find myself a prisoner-of-war; a most surprising position for a person who held two German letters of safe-conduct! Besides, I had been sent to Germany by a German Prince, which I could prove by his written instructions.

In due course I was interned and remained a prisoner until July 1916, in spite of nearly fifty applications for release. At long last I was exchanged and at the end of three months' leave was given a job at the War Office and did not get to the front till January 17th 1917.

According to letters that I have received from members of the late Court and others, the end of the Albanian Kingdom came suddenly. One night, some two or three weeks after I had left, the insurgents fired a few shells into the town, by way of a warning and then sent an ultimatum, demanding the Mbret's immediate departure from his realm, failing which they threatened to wipe out Durazzo. The till being empty and all hope of obtaining further funds having been abandoned, the King gave up all hope and, to avoid the risk of further bloodshed, decided to leave the country.[58]

As many exiles have done before him, he fled to Switzerland and took up his abode at Lugano, where he remained for some weeks. Later he returned to Germany, where, after some difficulties, he managed to get back into the army.

I hear that the King and Queen had to leave practically all they possessed at Durazzo, as their departure was more hurried than majestic. They put the palace and all their belongings under the protection of the Italian government and the latter, it is said, handed everything over to Essad Pasha, who once more appeared on the scene as soon as the King had left the country.

The same informant has written me the following rather amusing story, which shows that Essad had a sense of humour. The King sent orders to have all his things returned to Germany. For a long time he got no answer; at last some large packing cases arrived from Durazzo and it was hoped that they would contain the first instalment of household goods; on being opened it was discovered that they were full of newspapers, the children's toys and fire wood! An explanation was asked for and Essad is said to have answered very politely that he wanted everything else himself and that he had chosen this method of taking his revenge for the bombardment of his house.

Most of the King's ministers and other supporters had their properties destroyed or confiscated, and a large number went into exile, for a time, at least. Among these loyalists there were some honest, decent men, and it is sad to think that they too had to suffer for their loyalty to the throne! As to the unfortunate country itself, nobody can predict what is going to become of it; only one thing is certain and that is that the King will not go there again!

Often I think of the interesting time I spent in Albania and wish that I could get back there! It is an awful pity that the Albanian experiment failed; though the natives have many bad qualities, there is a lot of good in them.

Had the Great Powers sent a really strong man and given him their whole-hearted support, things would have turned out differently and the Albanian nation could have been saved from the avidity of its neighbours. The King was a broad-minded, generous man, but he was weak and could never make up his mind about anything; the people knew this and did not respect him. His kind-heartedness they took for weakness and his cautiousness they put down to fear. However his kindly character made him friends and had the Powers helped him, according to their undertakings, he might have pulled through. However the almighty Concert of Europe behaved disgracefully and failed to carry out any of its obligations; the Powers created the Kingdom, but as soon as they discovered that the Concert was a very doubtful quantity, they got tired of their new toy and put it aside. It is more than doubtful whether all the Powers at any time intended the Kingdom to be a success and I am under the impression that several of them were covertly hostile from the very beginning. It is certain that the Austrians intrigued for power, but they, at least had no designs on Albanian territory, like the Italians, Greeks, Serbians and Montenegrins. The Austrians wanted an independent, strong Albania with sympathy for the Austrian Empire, which would form a useful ally against the Serbians in case of war and for this reason they did everything in their power to support the King. I believe that the Austrians were our only real friends. Poor Albania!

NOTES

. . . . .

1   Libohova, who was born in 1882, was to have a long career in public life. In January 1931, as Court Chamberlain to King Zog during a visit to Vienna, he was shot in the leg during an assassination attempt on the King. He was generally very pro-Italian, and served as Prime Minister for two brief periods in 1943 during the Italian occupation of Albania. He died in Rome in about 1950. Vlora was born in Valona in 1885 into one of Albania's most powerful and wealthy families, died in Vienna in 1964. He, too, had a long career in public life, and was generally pro-Austrian. He wrote his memoirs in German (Lebenserinnerungen, which were published in Munich in 1973).

2   Konak is the Turkish word for a large house

3   Dr Gjergi Pekmezi (1872-1938) was later appointed as dragoman to the Austrian legation in Durazzo

4   These were Princess Louisa, born in 1880, who took a considerable interest in her brother's adventure in Albania, and Princess Elisabeth, who was born in 1883 and was an invalid for most of her life.

5   Waldenburg, about 30 miles south of Leipzig, then in the Kingdom of Saxony, was the home of the family of William of Wied wife, Princess Sophie Schonburg-Waldenburg.

6   This refers to William's elder brother, Frederick, 6th Prince of Wied (1872 -1945), the head of the family.

7   Bali was Essad's chief agent and the assassination referred to here took place in Scutari on 30 January 1913. Bali himself was assassinated in Tirana in September 1926 (J Swire, Albania - The Rise of a Kingdom, London, 1929, page 473)

8   Eustace La Trobe Leatham was Captain of HMS Gloucester from January 1909

9   For Faik Bey Konitza (1876-1942), see Faik Konitza, Selected

Correspondence, edited Bejtullah Destani (Centre for Albanian Studies, 2000)

10 17 March 1914, according to J Swire, Albania- The Rise of a Kingdom (page 200)

11 Hasan Bey Prishtina, born in 1873, was previously a Member of the Ottoman Parliament; he was a well-known leader of Albanians in Kosovo. He died in 1933. Dr Michael Tourtoulis, an Orthodox Christian who married a French woman, came to prominence by organising Prince Fuad of Egypt's unsuccessful campaign for the Albanian throne in December 1912. Lord Kitchener knew him in Cairo, and commented on his chameleon-like qualities (FO371/1891). In 1920, he was one of the four Regents of Albania.

12 The Sturdzas were an aristocratic Moldavian family; Prince Michel had a long career in the diplomatic service, and in 1940 was appointed Foreign Minister of Roumania in the first cabinet following the resignation of King Carol II. He continued as Foreign Minister to the Roumanian government in exile in 1945, and was energetically anti-communist. He gives a brief description of his time in Albania in his memoirs, The Suicide of Europe (Boston, 1968, page 13-14))

13 The Misurata was a yacht put at the King's disposal by the Italian Government; she had originally belonged to the Turkish Navy and had been captured by the Italians during the Tripoli War.

14 See Introduction, page xx. Reports sent to the Foreign Office in London stated she was sentenced to 15 years hard labour.

15 Sami Bey Vrioni (1876-1947) later played a part in the post-war reconstruction of Albania, serving as Minister of Agriculture in December 1918. He remained a monarchist, loyal to William of Wied (Swire, Albania, pages 285 & 443)

16 Christaki Zographos, a former Minister of Foreign Affairs for Greece, declared himself Prime Minister of the "Provisional Government" of Epirus at this time

17 This refers to the nomadic Vlach people of southern and central Albania, whose language was Latin and similar to Roumanian

18 "Black Hand" was an extreme nationalist movement in Serbia, led by army officers

19 Prince Luigi, Duke of Abruzzi, was born in 1873, a grandson of King Victor Emmanuel II of Italy. He was a well-known explorer before the First World War, and after the war developed banana plantations in Somalia. He died unmarried in 1933. (See Introduction, page xxxiv)

20 Abdi Bey Toptani (1864-1942) served as Minister of Finance in Kemal's first cabinet in November 1912; he was William of Wied's Minister of Agriculture and Commerce in May 1914, and was one of the four Regents, representing the Sunni Moslem community, in 1920 (Swire, Albania).

21 Leon Ghilardi was an adventurous soldier from Croatia, who became a close friend and advisor of King Zog. A huge, bearded man, he was a much admired figure in Albania until he was killed in revolt at Fieri in 1935 (see D R Oakley-Hill, An Englishman in Albania, Centre for Albanian Studies, 2002, page 79-80)

22 This almost certainly refers to Harold Sherwood Spencer, who was born in Wisconsin in 1890. In 1918 he was the main witness for the defence in an extraordinary case of criminal libel, R v Pemberton Billing, in which Spencer claimed he had been an ADC to King William in Albania in 1914, and that the king showed him a "Black Book" containing the names of 47,000 leading Englishmen who were homosexuals or perverts. Spencer fought bravely in Albania in 1914, but was shown to be a liar and mentally deranged in 1918.

23 Colonel Lodewijk WJK Thomson (born 1869) of the 12th Infantry Regiment of the Dutch Army was the ablest of the Dutch officers in Albania in 1914. Commissioned in 1888, he served first in the Dutch East Indies and then as an observer in the Boer War. He was elected Liberal MP for Leeuwarden in Holland, sitting in parliament between 1905 and 1913. He was a military observer at the siege of Janina, northern Greece in 1912, before being sent to Albania in November 1913 as second in command under General Willem J H de Veer. According to the most detailed analysis of the circumstances surrounding Thomson's death on 15 June 1914, he was probably killed by an unidentified Italian sniper, not by Moslem rebels (Gorrit T A Goslinga, The Dutch in Albania, Rome, 1972, pages 42-45)

24 Heaton-Armstrong adds a foot-note: "The British were very popular in Albania as the people still remember the time when we occupied the Ionian Islands, which we later handed over to Greece. The Corfiotes were very satisfied under British rule and it is said were exceedingly sorry when the British left the island; from there this sympathy spread to the mainland."

25 Heaton-Armstrong adds a foot-note: "Enquiries were afterwards made as to Captain Moltedo's antecedents and it was then discovered that he was a very efficient artillery officer, who had for some years served in the Congo."

26 General Willem J.H. de Veer, of the 3rd Regiment of Field Artillery in the Dutch Army, was the commanding officer of the 15 strong Dutch mission to Albania, appointed by the Conference of Ambassadors in London on 29 July 1913. Aged 56, he arrived in Valona on 10 November 1913, and left Albania on 7 August 1914 (Goslinga, The Dutch in Albania)

27 A different version of this incident is given in other sources, such as Edith Durham, Twenty Years of Balkan Tangle, pages 264-5; Swire, Albania, page 211-21, who partly relies on Prince Sturdza's account; Constantine Chekrezi, Albania Past and Present, page 150, and The Dutch in Albania, page 32. All these accounts assert that Sar, thinking he was about to be attacked by a small group of armed Moslems, ordered his men to open fire first. This was treated as a serious violation of the besa (Albanian for peace oath or truce) given by King William on his arrival in Albania, and justified the start of the rebellion.

28 Heaton-Armstrong adds a foot-note: "The Austrian Minister made it quite clear to the King that he would gladly allow the officers to come on land, on receiving a written request from him; however, though their services would have been very valuable, the King would not ask the Austrians for this favour; Austro-Italian jealousy would probably have caused complications."

29 William Walford was a businessman in Durazzo; he also manned the Austrian gun on this day, according to Swire, Albania, page 213

30 According to Swire, Albania, page 213, the royal family was taken aboard the Italian warship "Victor Pisani". Swire was apparently told this by William in correspondence in the 1920s. According to Goslinga, The Dutch in Albania, page 34, the Duke of Abruzzi, who commanded the "Misurata", hoisted the royal standard and sailed away from the coast as soon as the royal family was aboard.

31 Mehmed Pasha Dralla, a Kosovan, was a leader in rebellion against the Turks in July 1912, and served as Minister for War under Ismail Kemal in November 1912

32 Auguste Kral was later appointed Civil Administrator of northern Albania under Austro-Hungarian occupation in 1916

33 Harry Harling Lamb, born in 1857, had a long and distinguished career in the British consular service, serving as Vice-Consul in Scutari 1886-1894, then in Constantinople and Salonika, before being sent to Albania as the British representative of the International Commission of Control in Valona in 1913. He was

knighted in 1919 and died in 1948.

34 See Introduction pages xiii and xviii for Akif and Nogga.

35 Alessio is now Lezhe, a town near the coast of north Albania

36 He was Monsignor Louis Bumchi, a delegate to the Paris Peace Conference after the First World War, and one of the four members of the Regency Council appointed by the Albanian government in 1920: Swire, pages 285 and 313.

37 John Dunamace ("Jack") Heaton-Armstrong : see Introduction, pages xxi to xxxiii.

38 Ahmed Bey (1895-1961), the future King Zog, is called Mati here because he was chief of the Mati, a Moslem clan, whose territory lay to the north-east of Tirana. On about 10 May 1914 Ahmed had an audience with King William to discuss setting up a National Assembly. However, he had a quarrel with his kinsman, Essad, and Ahmed retired from court (Daily Mail, 30 May 1935).

39 The three men were Colonel Mauriccio, Captain Moltedo and Professor Chinigo : Swire, Albania, page 216.

40 These dated back to the Ottoman government, and provided diplomatic immunity.

41 Heaton-Armstrong adds this foot-note: "Baroness Amelie Godin was a Bavarian authoress, who has visited Albania for several years and has written about the country and its people in several chatty books. She spoke the language fluently and had an intimate knowledge of the Albanian character. She made herself very useful to the Austrian doctors in the Court hospital, interpreting for them and helping them to nurse the wounded. During the fights she showed the greatest pluck and looked after the men in the firing line. As she was known to be very Austrophile, she was not popular with the Italians, whom she cordially hated. Of course she was suspected of being an Austrian spy and her enemies even accused her of being in the Greek service. Though the King and Queen had reason to be grateful to her, she was very rarely seen at Court."

42 The long and distinguished career of Rear-Admiral Ernest Charles Thomas Troubridge CB, CMG, MVO(1862-1926)is described in The Dictionary of National Biography. For his role in the Serbian campaign of 1915, see CEJ Fryer, The Destruction of Serbia in 1915, (East European Monographs, 1997)

43 The Kastrati were one of five large Catholic tribes in northern Albania; their territory lay just to the north of Scutari, on the border with Montenegro (Edith Durham, High Albania, Chapter 3)

44 See Introduction page xxviii for her report to the Foreign Office

in London made the following day

45 Louis Gurakuchi, a Catholic, was an important figure. He was the
    first Principal of the Normal School in Elbasan in 1909, and
    served twice (in November 1912 and December 1918) as
    Minister of Education. Although a constitutional monarchist, he
    was a supporter of Fan Noli, and was Minister of Finance in his
    short-lived government in 1924. He was assassinated in Italy on
    2 March 1925 (Swire, Albania)

46 Heaton-Armstrong adds this foot-note: "A very cultured,
    studious type. Owing to the death of his brother he became head
    of the family and owner of the estate. But after the Second World
    War he lost everything to the East German Communists and
    eked out a living first as interpreter at the Law Court in Hanover,
    then as a French master at a school in the USA, finally returning
    to Salzburg, where we met again a short time before his death."

47 For Phillips, see Introduction, page xxviii

48 These were Captain Hugo J Verhulst and Lieutenant Hendrik G
    A Reimers, who were released by the rebels on 19 September
    1914 (Dutch in Albania, page 50)

49 The Laps were an Albanian tribe in the south-west of the
    country, around the port of Saranda, who had a warlike
    reputation

50 The "Lion of Janina" was the nickname given to Ali Pasha, born
    in 1740, the warlord who ruled with great harshness over Epirus,
    Thessaly and southern Albania between 1789 and his death in
    1822.

51 William Gurschner designed King William's flamboyant military
    uniforms and medals. Of the 1,000 men who originally enlisted
    under Gurschner, only 150 accompanied him to Durazzo, where
    they arrived on 4 July, according to Dutch in Albania, page 48

52 This meeting took place on 11 July in the palace at Durazzo

53 This almost certainly refers to a delegation of 15 "notables" from
    Valona and the surrounding area, led by Ismail Kemal, who
    returned to Albania on 30 June. Kemal wrote that King William
    "seemed incapable of making an observation or putting a
    question arising from his own personal thought. While I was
    explaining the different ways that might be adopted to get him
    out of his difficulties, he never once asked me how I thought of
    putting them into practice." (Memoirs of Ismail Kemal Bey, page
    384)

54 The Fustanella is a white pleated kilt, worn with leggings

55 see Introduction, page ix

56 Ferid Pasha Vlora (born 1859) was Grand Vizier of the Ottoman
    Empire 1903-1908. At the start of his reign King William invited
    Ferid to form his first government, but he declined (Swire,
    Albania, page 200)

57 The Bektashis were a Moslem sect, widespread throughout
    central and southern Albania, noted for their tolerant and
    generally pro-European views. Their adherents were mainly
    converts from Christianity, and they incorporated many
    Christian practices and traditions into their worship.

58 Valona surrendered to the rebels on 31 August. The next day, the
    rebels fired a few shots into the royal palace at Durazzo and
    demanded the King leave immediately. William's first plan was to
    go to Scutari and continue the fight there, but this was
    abandoned. On 2 September, William summoned his ministers
    and the three remaining members of International Commission
    of Control (from Austria and France, under the presidency of the
    Italian member, Count Carol Galli), and handed over control to
    them. On 3 September, King William and Queen Sophie locked
    up the palace, and embarked on the Italian ship "Misurati",
    bound for Venice (Denkschrift, pages 27-29)

SELECT BIBLIOGRAPHY AND SOURCES

. . . . .

NATIONAL ARCHIVES, LONDON:
ADM1 8386/210 & ADM1 8387/221 (Reports of Admiral
   Troubridge, June-July 1914)
FO320 3 & FO320 4 (International Commission of Control,
   1913-14)
FO371 1757 to FO371 1848 (Turkish Empire, 1913)
FO371 1885 to FO371 1896 (Albania, 1914)
FO371 128966 (Disposal of effects of late Madame Bunea in
   Roumania 1957)
FO881 10492 (Affairs of Albania, October to December 1913)
FO881 10594 (Affairs of Albania, January to March 1914)
IR104 24 (International Commission of Control)
British Documents on the Origins of the War, 1898-1914, edited G P
   Gooch & H Temperley (vols 9 to 11, HMSO, 1926-1938)

SOMERSET RECORD OFFICE, TAUNTON:
   Papers of Hon. Aubrey Herbert : DD/HER

PUBLISHED SOURCES
Almanac de Gotha (various editions)
Bridge, F R, *Great Britain and Austria-Hungary, 1906-1914: A
   Diplomatic History* (London, 1972)
Burgoyne, Elizabeth, *Carmen Sylva, Queen and Woman* (London,
   1941)
Burke's Landed Gentry of Great Britain (various editions)
Burke's Royal Families of the World (vol 1 Europe and Latin America,
   London, 1977)
Burke's Royal Families of the World (vol 2 Africa and the Middle
   East, London, 1980)
Chekrezi, Constantine A, *Albania, Past and Present* (New York, 1919)

Crampton, R J, *The Hollow Detente: Anglo-German Relations in the Balkans, 1911-1914* (London, 1979)

Dako, Christo A, *Albania: The Master Key to the Near East* (Boston, 1919)

Dillon, E J, "Albania's Tribulations and Colonel Phillips", "Albanian Characteristics"; "Benighted Condition of the Albanian People"; The Contemporary Review (vol 56, Jul-Dec 1914)

Durham, M Edith, *Twenty Years of Balkan Tangle* (London, 1920)

Durham, M Edith, *Albania and The Albanians, Selected Articles and Letters, 1903-1944*, edited Bejtullah Destani (Centre for Albanian Studies, London, 2001)

Ex-Kaiser William II, *My Memoirs, 1878-1918* (London, 1922)

Faik Konitza *Selected Correspondence*, edited Bejtullah Destani (Centre for Albania Studies, London, 2000)

Fischer, Bernd Jurgen, *King Zog and the Struggle for Stability in Albania* (Columbia University Press, 1984)

FitzHerbert, Margaret, *The Man Who Was Greenmantle* (London, 1983)

Goslinga, Gorrit T A, *The Dutch in Albania* (Rome, 1972)

Gottlieb, W W, *Studies in Secret Diplomacy* (London, 1957)

Helmreich, Ernest Christian, *The Diplomacy of the Balkan Wars, 1912-1913* (Cambridge, 1938)

Herbert, Aubrey, *Ben Kendim: A Record of Eastern Travel*, edited D MacCarthy (London, 1924)

Jelavich, C & B *The Establishment of the Balkan National States, 1804-1920* (Seattle, 1977)

Kondis, Basil, *Greece and Albania, 1908-1914* (Institute for Balkan Studies, vol 167, 1976)

Konitza, Faik, *Albania: The Rock Garden of Southeastern Europe and other Essays* (edited GM Panarity, Boston, 1957)

Maclehose, Olive, *Records of A Scotswoman, Katherine Stuart Macqueen, A Memoirs and Account of her work* (Glasgow, 1920)

Marie, Queen of Roumania, *The Story of My Life* (3 vols, London, 1934-5)

The Memoirs of Ismail Kemal Bey, edited Sommerville Story (London, 1920)

The Memoirs of Ismail Kemal Vlora and his work for the Independence of Albania, edited Renzo Falaschi (Tirana, 1997)

Pavlowitch, Stevan K, *A History of the Balkans 1804-1945* (London, 1999)

Perspectives on Albania, edited T Winnifrith (London, 1992)

Pribram, A F, *Austria-Hungary and Great Britain, 1908-1914* (Oxford, 1951)

Puto, Arben, *L'Independance Albanaise et la Diplomatie des Grandes Puissances, 1912 -1914* (Tirana, 1982)

Rankin, Lt-Col. Reginald, *The Inner History of the Balkan War* (London, 1914)

Ruvigny, Marquis of, *The Titled Nobility of Europe* (London, 1914)

Skendi, Stavro, *The Albanian National Awakening, 1878-1912* (Princeton, 1967)

Stavrianos, L S, *The Balkans since 1453* (New York, 1958)

Sturdza, Prince Michel, *The Suicide of Europe: Memoirs of Prince Michel Sturdza, former Foreign Minister of Rumania* (Boston, 1968)

Sulliotti, A Italo, *In Albania Sei Mesi di Regno Da Guglielmo di Wied a Essad Pascia* (Milan,1914)

Swire J, *Albania - The Rise of a Kingdom* (London, 1929)

Swire J, *King Zog's Albania* (London, 1937)

Vego, Milan N, *Austro-Hungarian Naval Policy, 1904-14* (London, 1996)

Vickers, Miranda, *The Albanians: A Modern History* (London, 1995)

Vlora, Ekrem Bey, *Lebenserinnerungen* (2 vols, Munich, 1973)

Who Was Who, 1916-1928; 1929-1940; 1941-1950

Wilhelm, Furst von Albanien, Prinz zu Wied, *Denkschrift uber Albanien* (privately printed in Berlin, 1917)

Woods, H Charles, *The Cradle of War* (Boston, 1918)

Zavalani, T, *History of Albania* (typed manuscript)

NEWSPAPERS
The Times
The Daily Mail
Le Figaro (21 March and 28 April 1913)
Literary Digest, 1913-1914
Illustrated London News, 1913-1914
The Spectator (3 May 1913)

INDEX

. . . . .